Table of contents

Hey there, amazing girl!

Welcome to your journey toward mastering your goals! This book is all about helping you set and achieve goals that matter to you, whether it's acing your next test, making the varsity team, starting a club, or becoming the best version of yourself. As a teen, you are in a unique stage of life where you are discovering who you are and what you want to become. Setting goals can be your secret weapon to navigating these exciting and sometimes challenging years. This book is here to guide you every step of the way.

Why Goals Matter in Your Life Right Now

You might be thinking, "Why should I care about setting goals? Isn't that something adults do?" The truth is, setting goals is even more important during your teenage years than at any other time. This is the time when you're figuring out your identity, exploring new interests, and laying the groundwork for your future. Having clear goals helps you make the most of this exciting time by giving you a sense of direction and purpose. It helps you focus on what really matters to you and gives you the confidence to chase after it.

Think of goal setting as a compass for your life's adventure. It helps you chart your course, navigate obstacles, and reach your desired destination. Without goals, it's easy to feel lost or overwhelmed by the many choices and challenges that come your way. But with the right goals, you have a roadmap that leads you toward the future you dream of, one step at a time.

How This Book Will Help You Achieve Your Dreams

This book isn't just about setting goals; it's about understanding the power you must shape your own life. We'll show you how to identify what's truly important to you, and how to turn those dreams into actionable steps. You'll learn how to set S.M.A.R.T. goals—goals that are Specific, Measurable, Achievable, Relevant, and Time-bound—and how to stay motivated and resilient, even when things don't go as planned.

Throughout this book, you'll find practical tips, inspiring stories, and interactive exercises designed to help you on your journey. You'll meet teens like Kaylie, who used goal setting to turn her grades around and build confidence in herself. You'll see how others have used these techniques to achieve their own dreams, whether it's starting a new hobby, excelling in sports, or becoming a leader in their school or community.

The Power of a Positive Mindset

Setting goals is also about believing in yourself and your ability to grow and succeed. A positive mindset is crucial to achieving your goals. This book will guide you in building that mindset, giving you tools to handle setbacks, learn from mistakes, and celebrate your successes. Remember, every step you take towards your goals is a step towards becoming the person you want to be

Are You Ready to Transform Your Life?

In the chapters ahead, we'll dive deep into what it means to set goals that align with your passions and values. You'll learn practical steps to take your dreams from "someday" to "now," and we'll share stories from other teens, like Kaylie, who have walked this path and achieved amazing things. Each chapter is packed with strategies to help you stay on track, maintain a positive attitude, and navigate the ups and downs of your journey.

This isn't just about achieving one goal—it's about developing the skills and mindset to set and reach goals throughout your life. Whether your goal is big or small, this book will help you build the habits and resilience you need to keep moving forward.

So, grab a notebook, open your mind, and get ready to discover the incredible power you have to shape your future. The journey to mastering your goals starts now, and I'm excited to be with you every step of the way.

Ready to start your journey to goal mastery? Let's go!!!

Charlene Parks

Introduction

The Importance of Goal Setting During Teenage Years

Setting goals is a powerful tool that can transform your teenage years. These years are a time of discovery, growth, and significant change. You are figuring out who you are, what you enjoy, and what kind of person you want to become. It's a journey that can sometimes feel overwhelming or uncertain. That's where goal setting comes in—it provides direction, focus, and a sense of purpose.

Why Goal Setting Matters Now More Than Ever

During your teenage years, you're navigating school, friendships, family dynamics, and personal interests—all while starting to think about your future. Goals help you make the most of this time by providing a roadmap to follow. When you set goals, you're choosing to take control of your path. Instead of drifting aimlessly, you're steering your life toward the things that matter most to you. This makes goal setting incredibly important during these formative years.

Setting goals also helps build essential life skills, like time management, perseverance, and resilience. By learning to set and achieve goals now, you are preparing yourself for future success in all areas of life, whether it's academics, sports, personal development, or career aspirations. It teaches you how to face challenges head-on and develop a positive mindset that will carry you through the ups and downs of life.

Overview of What You'll Learn in This Book

This book is designed to guide you step-by-step through the process of goal setting, helping you turn your dreams into reality. Here's what you can expect:

1. **Understanding Your Passions and Strengths**: Before setting any goals, it's crucial to know what excites you and what you're good at. We'll help you explore your interests and strengths to identify the areas where goal setting will have the most impact.
2. **Mastering the S.M.A.R.T. Goal-Setting Method**: You'll learn about the S.M.A.R.T. method—a powerful technique to create Specific, Measurable, Achievable, Relevant, and Time-bound goals. This chapter will teach you how to define clear goals that you can realistically achieve.
3. **Building a Personalized Goal Blueprint**: Once you have your goals in mind, we'll show you how to create a detailed action plan to achieve them. This includes breaking down your goals into manageable steps, setting deadlines, and tracking your progress.

4. **Maintaining a Positive Mindset**: A positive attitude is key to achieving your goals. You'll learn strategies to stay motivated, handle setbacks, and celebrate your progress along the way.

5. **Overcoming Challenges and Building Resilience**: We'll discuss common obstacles you might face on your journey and provide practical strategies to overcome them. Building resilience is all about learning from your experiences and continuing to push forward.

6. **Time Management for Goal Achievement**: Effective time management is crucial for reaching your goals. We'll provide tips on how to balance school, extracurricular activities, and personal time while staying focused on your objectives.

7. **Creating a Support Network**: You don't have to achieve your goals alone. We'll explore how to build a support system of friends, family, mentors, and peers who can help you stay motivated and accountable.

8. **Celebrating Success and Planning for the Future**: Finally, we'll show you how to celebrate your achievements and reflect on your journey. You'll also learn how to set new goals and continue your growth beyond this book.

Introducing Kaylie

Throughout this book, you'll meet teens like Kaylie, who turned her struggles into success by setting clear, actionable goals. Kaylie was struggling with her math grades, feeling overwhelmed and unsure about her abilities. But instead of giving up, she decided to take control of her situation. By setting a specific goal to improve her math grade from a C to an A, Kaylie created a plan, sought help when needed, and stayed committed to her goal. Her journey wasn't easy, but her determination and the strategies she learned made a huge difference in her confidence and academic performance.

Kaylie's story is just one example of how powerful goal setting can be. You'll also read about other teens who have used similar techniques to overcome challenges, achieve their dreams, and grow into confident, capable young adults. These stories are here to inspire you and show you that no matter where you start, you can achieve great things with the right mindset and tools.

By the end of this book, you'll have everything you need to set and achieve your own goals, no matter how big or small. You'll learn how to turn your dreams into actionable plans and navigate the journey of achieving them with confidence and resilience. Whether you want to improve your grades, learn a new skill, or take on a leadership role, this book will provide you with the guidance and support you need to succeed.

Let's get started on this exciting journey together. Remember, goal setting isn't just about reaching a destination—it's about discovering your potential and becoming the best version of yourself. Ready to take the first step toward mastering your goals?

Chapter 1: What is Goal Mastery?

Understanding Goals vs. Dreams

We all have dreams—those big, exciting, visions of what we want our lives to be like. Dreams are the seeds of our desires, the things we imagine when we think about our future. Maybe you dream of becoming a famous artist, starting your own business, or traveling the world. Dreams are important because they inspire us and give us something to look forward to. But here's the thing: dreams on their own are just that—dreams. Without action, they remain ideas floating in our minds, untapped and unrealized.

Goals, on the other hand, are the bridges that connect our dreams to reality. Goals are specific, actionable steps we take to make our dreams come true. While a dream might be to "become a successful writer," a goal would be "to write and publish three short stories by the end of the year." Goals take the abstract nature of dreams and turn them into tangible, achievable outcomes. Understanding the difference between a dream and a goal is the first step toward goal mastery.

Think of it this way: Dreams are like the destination on a map, while goals are the roads that lead you there. Both are essential, but you need goals to guide you on the journey and ensure you're moving in the right direction.

The Difference Between Setting Goals and Mastering Goals

Setting goals is the first step toward achieving your dreams, but mastering goals takes it to the next level. Anyone can set a goal, but mastering goals involves understanding how to effectively plan, execute, and adjust your actions to reach that goal. It's about developing the skills and mindset needed to not only reach your goals but to keep growing and setting new ones throughout your life.

Mastering goals means being proactive rather than reactive. It's about taking control of your future by carefully planning your actions and staying committed, even when things get tough. It involves setting clear, specific goals, creating a plan to achieve them, and being flexible enough to adapt as needed. Goal mastery is about persistence, resilience, and continuous improvement.

When you master your goals, you're not just working toward a single outcome—you're building a lifelong habit of success. You learn how to set goals that are meaningful and aligned with your values, and you develop the confidence to pursue them with determination. Mastering goals means you're always moving forward, learning from your experiences, and becoming the best version of yourself.

Discovering Your Passions and Strengths

Before you can set effective goals, it's important to understand what truly excites you and where your strengths lie. Your passions are the activities, subjects, or causes that you care deeply about. They're the things that make you feel energized, motivated, and fulfilled. Your strengths are the skills and abilities you naturally excel at. Together, your passions and strengths provide a powerful foundation for goal setting.

When your goals align with your passions and strengths, they become more meaningful and motivating. You're more likely to stay committed to your goals when they reflect who you are and what you care about. This is why it's so important to take the time to explore your interests and identify what makes you unique.

Start by asking yourself a few questions:

- What activities do I lose track of time doing?
- What subjects do I enjoy learning about the most?
- What causes or issues am I passionate about?
- What skills do I naturally excel at or receive compliments on?

_____

_____

_____

_____

_____

_____

By reflecting on these questions, you can start to identify the areas of your life where you might want to set goals. This self-awareness will help you set goals that are both fulfilling and achievable.

Why Goal Setting is Important

Goal setting is a powerful tool for creating the life you want. It gives you direction, focus, and a sense of purpose. When you set goals, you're making a conscious decision to take control of your life and work toward something meaningful. Let's explore some of the key reasons why goal setting is so important.

Benefits of Having Clear Goals

1. **Provides Direction**: Clear goals act as a roadmap, guiding your actions and decisions. They help you focus on what's important and prevent you from getting sidetracked by distractions. When you know where you're going, it's easier to make choices that align with your desired outcomes.
2. **Increases Motivation**: Goals give you something to strive for. They provide a sense of purpose and a reason to push through challenges. When you have a clear goal in mind, you're more likely to stay motivated and committed to achieving it.
3. **Boosts Confidence**: Achieving goals, no matter how small, boosts your confidence and self-esteem. Each success reinforces the belief that you're capable of achieving even more. Setting and reaching goals helps you build a positive self-image and develop a "can-do" attitude.
4. **Encourages Growth**: Goal setting pushes you to step out of your comfort zone and try new things. It challenges you to grow, learn, and improve. By setting goals, you're constantly working on becoming a better version of yourself.

Overcoming the Fear of Failure

One of the biggest obstacles to setting goals is the fear of failure. It's natural to worry about not succeeding or making mistakes along the way. However, failure is a part of the learning process and can actually be a steppingstone to success. When you set goals, it's important to embrace the possibility of failure as an opportunity for growth.

Instead of seeing failure as a negative outcome, view it as a chance to learn and improve. Every setback provides valuable lessons that can help you adjust your approach and move closer to your goals. By overcoming the fear of failure, you open yourself up to new possibilities and build the resilience needed to achieve your dreams.

Kaylie's Story: How She Used Goals to Improve Her Grades

Kaylie's story is a perfect example of how goal setting can lead to personal growth and success. Kaylie was struggling with her math grades, which affected her confidence and made her feel overwhelmed. Instead of giving up, she decided to take control of the situation by setting a clear goal: to improve her math grade from a C to an A by the end of the semester.

Kaylie's goal was specific, measurable, and time-bound, which made it easier for her to create a plan to achieve it. She started by identifying the areas where she needed help and sought out resources like tutoring and extra practice. She broke down her goal into smaller steps, such as studying for an hour each day and completing all her homework assignments on time.

Throughout the semester, Kaylie stayed committed to her goal, even when she faced challenges. She tracked her progress, celebrated small victories, and adjusted her plan when needed. By the end of the semester, Kaylie not only improved her math grade but also gained a new sense of confidence and pride in her abilities.

Kaylie's story shows that with the right mindset, clear goals, and a solid plan, you can achieve great things—even when the odds seem stacked against you.

Now that you understand the power of turning dreams into actionable goals and the importance of aligning them with your passions and strengths, it's time to take the first step on your journey to goal mastery. Before you can set meaningful goals, you need to uncover what truly excites and motivates you. Let's take a moment to reflect on your unique talents, interests, and values—because understanding these will serve as the foundation for every goal you set. Ready to dive in? Let's start discovering what makes you, *you*!

By answering the following questions, you'll gain a clearer understanding of what excites you and where your strengths lie. Use these insights to start thinking about the goals you want to set for yourself.

This chapter lays the foundation for your goal-setting journey. You've learned the difference between goals and dreams, the importance of mastering your goals, and how to align your goals with your passions and strengths. You've also been introduced to Kaylie's inspiring story and completed a reflection activity to help you identify your own goals. In the next chapter, you'll learn how to turn your dreams into actionable goals using the S.M.A.R.T. method. Let's continue this journey toward mastering your goals!

Reflection Activity: Identifying Your Passions and Strengths

Instructions: Take a few minutes to reflect on the following questions and write down your thoughts.

1. **What activities or subjects do I enjoy the most?**

_____

_____

_____

2. **What skills do I naturally excel at?**

_____

_____

_____

3. **What causes or issues am I passionate about?**

_____

_____

_____

4. **What challenges have I overcome in the past that I am proud of?**

_____

_____

_____

5. **What would I like to achieve in the next year?**

_____

_____

_____

Chapter 2: Dream Big, Plan Smart – The S.M.A.R.T. Way

Now, let's talk about the S.M.A.R.T. goal-setting method. S.M.A.R.T. stands for Specific, Measurable, Achievable, Relevant, and Time-bound. These five steps are like a road map to help you define what you want to achieve clearly and stay on track.

Have you ever set a goal that felt impossible to achieve? Maybe it was to ace a math test, win a soccer championship, or learn to play the guitar. If so, you're not alone! The problem is not your dreams but the lack of a clear plan to achieve them. That's where S.M.A.R.T. goals come in.

S.M.A.R.T. goals are like a treasure map for your dreams. They make your goals clear, actionable, and within reach. This chapter will guide you through each part of the S.M.A.R.T. process so you can turn your big ideas into achievable steps—and crush them!

Kaylie's S.M.A.R.T. Goal Example

Kaylie's goal was specific: she wanted to improve her math grade from a C to an A. She made it measurable by tracking her test scores and homework grades. To make it achievable, Kaylie set up a study schedule and got help from a tutor. Her goal was relevant because it aligned with her desire to feel more confident in school and prepare for advanced courses. Finally, she made it time-bound by setting a deadline to achieve her goal by the end of the semester.

Let's break it down further:

- **Specific**: Know exactly what you want. Kaylie knew she wanted to raise her math grade.
- **Measurable**: Make sure you can track your progress. Kaylie tracked her test and homework scores.
- **Achievable**: Set a goal that is challenging but realistic. Kaylie knew she could improve with a better study schedule and help from a tutor.
- **Relevant**: Choose goals that matter to you. For Kaylie, improving her math grade was crucial for her self-confidence and academic future.
- **Time-bound**: Set a deadline. Kaylie's deadline was the end of the semester.

Breaking Down the S.M.A.R.T. Framework

	Focus Your Goal	Activity / Action
Specific	A specific goal answers questions like "What do I want to achieve?" and "Why does this matter?" Example: Instead of saying, "I want to get fit," say, "I want to run a mile in under 10 minutes."	Think of a goal you have and make it specific. Use prompts like: • What exactly do I want to achieve? • Why is this important to me? • Who can help me?

	Focus Your Goal	Activity / Action
Measurable	A measurable goal lets you see your progress, which keeps you motivated. Example: Instead of saying, "I want to read more books," say, "I will read two books per month.	Pick a goal and add a measurable component. For example, "Complete 20 minutes of math practice daily" or "Score at least 80% on weekly quizzes."

⭐ **Pro Tip:** Celebrate small wins! Reward yourself when you hit milestones.

	Focus Your Goal	Activity / Action
Achievable	Your goal should stretch you but still be within reach. Unrealistic goals can lead to frustration, while achievable goals build confidence. **Example:** Instead of "I want to become fluent in French in three months," say, "I want to learn 20 new French phrases each week for the next three months."	Write down your goal and any obstacles that might get in the way. Then, list solutions to overcome those challenges.
	Focus Your Goal	**Activity / Action**
Relevant	Your goal should connect to your passions or long-term plans. A relevant goal feels meaningful and worth pursuing. **Example:** If you love animals, a relevant goal could be, "Volunteer at an animal shelter for two hours every Saturday."	Ask yourself, "How does this goal fit into what I want for my future?" If it doesn't, tweak it to align with your bigger dreams.
	Focus Your Goal	**Activity / Action**
Time-bound	A deadline creates urgency and keeps you on track. **Example:** Instead of "I want to finish my project," say, "I will complete my project by March 15."	**Activity:** Break your goal into smaller milestones with deadlines. For example: • Week 1: Research the topic. • Week 2: Write the outline. • Week 3: Complete the first draft. • Week 4: Edit and submit.

Real-Life Examples of S.M.A.R.T. Goals

Example 1: Improving Grades

- **Specific:** Improve my history grade from a C to a B.
- **Measurable:** Track test and assignment scores.
- **Achievable:** Study for 30 minutes daily and attend tutoring once a week.
- **Relevant:** Higher grades will help me qualify for advanced classes.
- **Time-bound:** Achieve this by the end of the semester.

Example 2: Becoming More Active

- **Specific:** Run a mile in under 9 minutes.
- **Measurable:** Track my running time each week.
- **Achievable:** Practice running three times a week after school.
- **Relevant:** I want to be in shape for soccer tryouts.
- **Time-bound:** Achieve this within eight weeks.

Real-Life Case Studies

- **Case Study 1:** Sophia, a high school soccer player, wanted to increase her endurance. Her S.M.A.R.T. goal was: "Run 2 miles in under 18 minutes by practicing three times a week for two months." By sticking to her plan, she improved her endurance and reached her goal in just six weeks.

- **Case Study 2:** Liam, a musician, wanted to master a new song on the piano. His S.M.A.R.T. goal was: "Practice 30 minutes daily and perform the song for my family by March 15." Breaking the song into manageable sections made the goal less overwhelming.

Now that you know how to create S.M.A.R.T. goals, it's time to act! Remember, every big achievement starts with a small, specific step. Whether your goal is to ace a test, learn a new skill, or build confidence, the S.M.A.R.T. framework will guide you every step of the way. Write your first S.M.A.R.T. goal and start turning your dreams into reality!

Activity: Create Your Own S.M.A.R.T. Goal

Think about something you really want to achieve, just like Kaylie did with her math grade. Use the steps we just discussed to create your own S.M.A.R.T. goal using the following worksheet.

SMART GOALS PLANNER

Identify a goal that is specific, measurable, achievable, relevant, and time-bound (SMART). Break it into actionable steps, each with its own deadline.

S — Specific

What exactly do you want to achieve?

M — Measurable

How will you track your advancement?

A — Attainable

Evaluate the feasibility of your goal.

R — Relevant

How does it fit into your broader objectives?

T — Time-bound

What is the deadline?

Reflection Activity

Reflect on a time(s) you set a goal but didn't achieve it. Which part of S.M.A.R.T. could have made the difference?

_____

_____

_____

_____

_____

_____

_____

_____

_____

_____

_____

_____

_____

_____

_____

_____

_____

_____

_____

Chapter 3: Creating Your Personal Goal Blueprint

Achieving success isn't just about working hard—it's about working smart. That means having a clear sense of who you are, where you want to go, and how you plan to get there. This chapter will guide you through creating your personal goal blueprint—a detailed plan that outlines your mission, vision, values, and actionable steps for success.

Your blueprint will serve as a roadmap, helping you stay focused and motivated, even when challenges arise. As you work through this chapter, you'll find questions and prompts designed to inspire self-reflection and creativity. Let's start building your future, one step at a time.

The Importance of a Goal Blueprint

A goal blueprint is essential because it transforms your goals from abstract ideas into concrete actions. It gives you clarity on what needs to be done, helps you stay organized, and keeps you motivated by showing you the path forward. With a blueprint, you can:

1. **Visualize Your Path**: Knowing the steps to reach your goal makes the journey less daunting and more manageable. When you can see the entire path laid out in front of you, it's easier to stay focused and motivated, even when the journey gets tough.
2. **Stay Focused**: A blueprint helps you concentrate on what matters most. It serves as a constant reminder of your priorities, preventing you from getting sidetracked by distractions or less important tasks. With a clear plan, you can maintain your momentum and stay on track toward achieving your goals.
3. **Track Progress**: With clear steps and milestones, you can easily see how far you've come and what still needs to be done. This boosts your motivation and helps you stay committed because you're able to celebrate your progress along the way. Tracking your progress also allows you to adjust as needed, ensuring that you're always moving in the right direction.
4. **Adapt and Adjust**: Life is unpredictable, and sometimes things don't go as planned. A blueprint allows you to make necessary adjustments without losing sight of your goal. If an obstacle arises, you can revisit your plan, make changes, and continue moving forward. This flexibility is crucial for maintaining momentum and achieving your goals, no matter what challenges you face.

By building a personal goal blueprint, you're setting yourself up for success. You're taking the time to think through your goals and create a strategic plan to achieve them. This careful planning will not only help you reach your goals but also teach you valuable skills in organization, problem-solving, and perseverance.

Building a goal blueprint involves several key steps. Let's walk through each one so you can create a comprehensive plan for reaching your goals.

Create Your Blueprint

Step 1: Define Your Mission Statement

Your mission is your purpose. It's what drives you to get up each day and strive for more. A strong mission statement captures the impact you want to make and the person you aspire to be.

 ### What Is a Mission Statement?

A mission statement defines your "why." It answers the question: What do you want to achieve in life, and what impact do you want to make? It is the foundation for all your goals and decisions.

Reflection Questions:

- What are you passionate about?
- How do you want to contribute to your family, school, or community?
- What motivates you to do your best?

Example Mission Statement: "To help my community by becoming a leader who inspires others to dream big."

Use the **Mission Statement** section of the worksheet to write your mission below. Take your time to craft something that resonates with your values and purpose.

Step 2: Define Your Vision Statement

Your vision is the big picture. It's what you hope to achieve in the next 5-10 years. Building on the SMART goals you set in Chapter 2, this step will help you connect those goals to a broader, long-term purpose

 ### Why Is a Vision Statement Important?

A vision statement serves as your "north star." It provides direction and keeps you focused on the bigger picture, even when you face obstacles.

Reflection Questions:

- Where do you see yourself in five years? Ten years?
- How do your current goals contribute to your long-term aspirations?
- What does success look like for you?

Example Vision Statement: "To graduate with honors, start a successful career, and give back to my community."

Write your vision in the **Vision Statement** section of the worksheet. Be bold and dream big—your vision should inspire and excite you.

Step 3: Define Your Core Values

Your core values are the principles that guide your decisions and actions. Knowing your values will help you make choices that align with your goals.

 ## Why Are Core Values Important?

Core values act as your moral compass. They ensure your actions and decisions stay true to who you are, even when faced with challenges.

Reflection Questions:

- What qualities do you admire in others?
- Which values matter most to you in school, relationships, or work?
- How do you want to be remembered by others?

Examples of Core Values:

- Integrity - **being honest and having strong moral principles. It means doing the right thing, even when no one is watching.**
    - **In Practice**: Keeping your promises, being truthful in your words and actions, and staying consistent with your values.

- Growth - **the process of continuously improving yourself, learning new skills, and striving to be better than you were yesterday.**
    - **In Practice**: Seeking out opportunities to learn, embracing challenges as opportunities to improve, and being open to constructive feedback.

- Empathy - **the ability to understand and share the feelings of others. It involves seeing situations from someone else's perspective and showing compassion.**
  - o **In Practice**: Listening without judgment, offering support when others are struggling, and taking time to understand someone else's experiences or emotions.

- Determination - **the drive and perseverance to achieve your goals, even in the face of difficulties or obstacles.**
  - o **In Practice**: Staying focused on your objectives, working hard to overcome challenges, and refusing to give up when things get tough.

- Gratitude - **the practice of recognizing and appreciating the good things in life, both big and small, and expressing thankfulness for them.**
  - o **In Practice**: Taking time to acknowledge the people and experiences that bring you joy, saying "thank you" often, and focusing on the positives even in difficult situations.

Write 3-5 core values in the **Core Values** section of the worksheet. These will serve as your compass as you work toward your goals.

Step 4: Refine Your Goals

Now that you have your mission and vision in mind, revisit the SMART goals you set earlier. This step will help you refine and align those goals with your broader vision and mission.

How to Refine Your Goals: Refining your goals involves breaking them down into actionable steps and ensuring they remain relevant and achievable as your circumstances evolve.

Reflection Questions:

- Are your goals still relevant to your long-term vision?
- Do they challenge you to grow while remaining achievable?
- How can you break down these goals into even smaller, actionable steps?

Example Refined Goal: Original: "Achieve a B in math this semester." Refined: "Study math for 30 minutes daily, complete all homework on time, and attend weekly tutoring sessions to achieve a B in math this semester."

Write your refined goals in the **Refined Goals** section of the worksheet. Focus on clarity and precision to set yourself up for success.

Step 5: Actionable Steps

Big dreams start with small steps. To bring your mission and vision to life, you need to set actionable goals. Think about the first steps you can take to start your journey.

Breaking Down Your Goals: Breaking your goals into smaller steps makes them more manageable and helps you build momentum as you achieve each milestone.

Reflection Questions:

- What small actions can you take this month to move closer to your vision?
- How can you break larger goals into smaller, manageable steps?
- What resources or tools can help you along the way?

Example Actionable Steps:

1. Join a study group.
2. Set a daily schedule.
3. Find a mentor to guide you.

Write your first three actionable steps in the **Actionable Steps** section of the worksheet.

Step 6: Support System

No one achieves success alone. Your support system includes the people who encourage, guide, and help you stay accountable.

Building Your Support System: Identify the people or groups who can help you stay motivated and provide guidance when you need it most.

Reflection Questions:

- Who inspires and motivates you?
- Who can you rely on for advice or support?
- How can you strengthen your relationships with these people?

Example Support System:

- My teacher
- My best friend
- My older sister

List your support system in the **Support System** section of the worksheet. Remember to thank them for their encouragement and support!

Kaylie's Action Plan: A Step-by-Step Guide

To help illustrate how to build a goal blueprint, let's look at Kaylie's action plan for improving her math grades. Kaylie's goal was to raise her math grade from a C to an A by the end of the semester. Here's how she created her personal goal blueprint:

1. **Define the Big Goal**: Kaylie's big goal was to improve her math grade from a C to an A by the end of the semester. She knew this goal was important to her because it would boost her confidence, improve her overall GPA, and prepare her for future coursework.
2. **Break Down the Goal into Actionable Steps**:
   o **Daily Study Routine**: Kaylie committed to studying math for 30 minutes each day after school. She found a quiet space in her home where she could focus without distractions and made a habit of reviewing her notes and practice problems daily.
   o **Homework Completion**: Kaylie decided to complete all math homework assignments on time and thoroughly. She set aside time each evening to work on her homework and made sure to double-check her work for accuracy.
   o **Extra Practice**: To reinforce her learning, Kaylie used online resources and practice problems to get additional practice. She found websites and apps that offered interactive math exercises and made it a point to complete a few extra problems each week.
   o **Seek Help**: Kaylie recognized that she needed additional support, so she arranged to attend weekly tutoring sessions and ask her teacher for clarification on any difficult topics. She also made it a habit to ask questions in class and seek help from her peers when needed.
   o **Join a Study Group**: Kaylie joined a study group with her classmates to review material and prepare for tests. The group met twice a week, and Kaylie found that discussing math concepts with others helped her better understand the material.
3. **Set Deadlines and Milestones**:
   o **First Milestone**: Raise her math grade to a B by the midterm. Kaylie set this milestone to assess her progress halfway through the semester and make any necessary adjustments to her plan.
   o **Second Milestone**: Complete all homework and quizzes with at least 85% accuracy by the end of each week. This milestone helped Kaylie stay on track with her daily and weekly tasks and ensured she was making steady progress.

- **Final Deadline**: Achieve an A by the end of the semester. This was Kaylie's ultimate goal, and she used it as a guiding star to stay focused and motivated throughout the semester.

4. **Track Progress and Adjust as Needed**:
   - **Weekly Check-Ins**: Every Sunday, Kaylie reviewed her progress from the past week and adjusted her study plan if necessary. If she noticed she was struggling with a particular topic, she would allocate extra study time to that area or seek additional help from her tutor.
   - **Celebrate Milestones**: Kaylie rewarded herself with a fun activity, like watching a movie or hanging out with friends, after achieving each milestone. This helped her stay motivated and provided a sense of accomplishment along the way.

By following this action plan, Kaylie stayed focused and made steady progress toward her goal. She was able to identify exactly what needed to be done and when, which helped her manage her time effectively and stay on track. Her clear blueprint allowed her to see her progress, celebrate her successes, and stay motivated, even when faced with challenges.

PERSONAL GOALS BLUEPRINT

This worksheet is designed to help you build your Personal Goal Blueprint. Use it to clarify your mission, vision, core values, and actionable steps while identifying milestones and support systems that will guide you to success.

Step 1: Mission Statement

What to Do: *Define your mission by identifying your purpose and what motivates you. Think about the impact you want to make and what drives you to achieve your goals.*

Step 2: Vision Statement

What to Do: *Imagine your ideal future. Where do you see yourself in 5-10 years? Your vision should align with your long-term goals and inspire you to keep moving forward.*

Step 3: Core Values

What to Do: *List the principles that guide your decisions and actions. Reflect on what is most important to you and how it influences your goals.*

Step 4: Refine Your Goals

What to Do: *Revisit the SMART goals you created in Chapter 2. Break them into smaller, actionable steps that make your goals more achievable and aligned with your vision.*
Example Refined Goal: Original: *"Achieve a B in math this semester."Example Refined Goal: Original: "Achieve a B in math this semester."*

PERSONAL GOALS BLUEPRINT

Step 5: Actionable Steps

What to Do: *Identify the specific steps you'll take to accomplish your refined goals. Think about small, manageable actions you can complete daily or weekly.*

Step 6: Support System

What to Do: *Identify the people who will support you on your journey. These could be mentors, friends, family members, or teachers who can provide encouragement and guidance.*

Reflection Activity: Visualizing Your Goal Journey

Take a moment to close your eyes and visualize yourself achieving your goal. Imagine every detail—what you're doing, how you feel, and who is with you. Think about the steps you took to get there and the obstacles you overcame along the way.

Write down your thoughts and feelings about this visualization:

1. **How did it feel to achieve your goal?**

   _____

   _____

   _____

2. **What steps were most important in reaching your goal?**

   _____

   _____

   _____

3. **What challenges did you face, and how did you overcome them?**

   _____

   _____

   _____

4. **What support did you receive, and how did it help you?**

   _____

   _____

   _____

By visualizing your goal journey, you're preparing your mind for success. This exercise helps reinforce your commitment and boosts your confidence in your ability to achieve your goals. Visualization is a powerful tool that allows you to see your success before it happens, making it easier to stay focused and motivated on your path to goal mastery.

Building your personal goal blueprint is an essential step in mastering your goals. By defining your big goals, breaking them down into actionable steps, setting deadlines, and visualizing your journey, you are setting yourself up for success. Remember, goal mastery isn't just about reaching the destination—it's about enjoying the journey and growing along the way.

Chapter 4: The Power of a Positive Mindset

Your mindset is one of the most powerful tools you have in achieving your goals. It shapes how you see the world, how you approach challenges, and how you bounce back from setbacks. In this chapter, we'll explore why mindset matters so much, how to develop a growth mindset, and practical techniques for staying positive as you work towards your goals. We'll also take a look at how Kaylie used her positive mindset to overcome challenges, and we'll provide activities and reflections to help you strengthen your own mindset.

Why Mindset Matters

Your mindset is the set of beliefs and attitudes you hold about yourself and your abilities. It's the lens through which you view your experiences and the world around you. A positive mindset can empower you to take on new challenges, push through difficult times, and keep striving toward your goals, while a negative mindset can hold you back, making it harder to overcome obstacles and maintain motivation.

There are two primary types of mindsets: a **fixed mindset** and a **growth mindset**.

- **Fixed Mindset**: People with a fixed mindset believe that their abilities, intelligence, and talents are fixed traits—they're either born with them or not. This mindset can make people afraid to try new things or push themselves because they fear failure or judgment. If they don't succeed right away, they may give up, believing they're not capable of improvement.
- **Growth Mindset**: In contrast, people with a growth mindset believe that abilities and intelligence can be developed through hard work, effort, and learning. They see challenges as opportunities to grow and view failure as a valuable part of the learning process. This mindset encourages perseverance, resilience, and a love of learning.

A growth mindset is crucial for achieving your goals because it encourages you to embrace challenges, learn from your mistakes, and keep going, even when things are tough. When you believe that you can improve and grow, you're more likely to put in the effort required to achieve your goals.

Developing a Growth Mindset

Developing a growth mindset is all about changing the way you think about yourself and your abilities. It involves recognizing that your brain is like a muscle—it gets stronger with use and practice. Here are some strategies to help you develop a growth mindset:

1. **Embrace Challenges**: View challenges as opportunities to learn and grow. Instead of avoiding difficult tasks, approach them with curiosity and a willingness to learn. Remind yourself that every challenge you face is an opportunity to become stronger and more skilled.
2. **Learn from Mistakes**: Understand that mistakes are a natural part of the learning process. When you make a mistake, don't see it as a failure. Instead, ask yourself what you can learn from it and how you can improve next time. This attitude will help you turn setbacks into stepping stones for success.
3. **Celebrate Effort, Not Just Results**: Recognize and celebrate the effort you put into your work, regardless of the outcome. This reinforces the idea that effort leads to improvement and helps build resilience. Praise yourself and others for hard work, dedication, and perseverance, rather than just the final result.
4. **Replace Negative Thoughts with Positive Ones**: Pay attention to your inner dialogue. When you catch yourself thinking, "I can't do this" or "I'm not good enough," challenge those thoughts and replace them with positive affirmations like, "I can learn how to do this" or "I am capable of improving." Over time, this practice will help shift your mindset to be more growth oriented.
5. **Surround Yourself with Positivity**: Spend time with people who encourage and support your growth. Positive influences can inspire you to maintain a growth mindset, while negative influences may reinforce a fixed mindset. Choose friends, mentors, and role models who believe in continuous learning and self-improvement.
6. **Keep a Learning Mindset**: Always be open to learning new things. Take on new hobbies, read books, or learn a new skill. The more you push yourself to learn and grow, the more naturally a growth mindset will come to you.

By developing a growth mindset, you'll be better equipped to handle the ups and downs of life and stay committed to your goals, no matter what challenges come your way

Techniques for Staying Positive: Visualization, Affirmations, and Gratitude

Staying positive is crucial for maintaining motivation and perseverance as you work toward your goals. Here are three powerful techniques that can help you stay positive and focused:

1. **Visualization**: Visualization is the practice of imagining yourself achieving your goals. It's a powerful tool that helps you stay focused on your desired outcome and motivates you to keep moving forward. When you visualize, try to imagine every detail—how you feel, what you see, and who is with you. This practice can help you build confidence and reduce anxiety about the future.
   - **How to Practice Visualization**: Find a quiet space where you won't be disturbed. Close your eyes and take a few deep breaths to relax. Then, picture yourself achieving your goal. Imagine the sights, sounds, and feelings associated with your success. Spend a few minutes each day visualizing your success to keep yourself motivated and focused.
2. **Affirmations**: Affirmations are positive statements that you repeat to yourself to build confidence and a positive mindset. They help reframe negative thoughts and reinforce your belief in your abilities. By regularly practicing affirmations, you can train your mind to focus on your strengths and potential rather than your limitations.
   - **How to Create Affirmations**: Think about the qualities or achievements you want to reinforce. Write down a few positive statements in the present tense, such as "I am capable of achieving my goals" or "I am resilient and strong." Repeat these affirmations to yourself daily, especially when you're facing challenges or feeling discouraged.
3. **Gratitude**: Practicing gratitude involves focusing on the positive aspects of your life and appreciating what you have. Gratitude helps shift your mindset from what you lack to what you have, fostering a sense of contentment and positivity. By regularly acknowledging the good things in your life, you can maintain a more optimistic outlook and reduce stress and anxiety.
   - **How to Practice Gratitude**: Each day, take a few moments to write down three things you're grateful for. These can be big or small—anything from a supportive friend to a sunny day. Reflect on why you're grateful for these things and how they make you feel. This practice can help you cultivate a more positive mindset and improve your overall well-being.

Kaylie's Positive Mindset: Overcoming Challenges with Optimism

Kaylie's journey to improving her math grades wasn't easy. She faced many challenges along the way, from difficult math concepts to moments of self-doubt. However, Kaylie was able to maintain a positive mindset throughout her journey, which played a crucial role in her success.

Kaylie used several techniques to stay positive:

1. **Embracing Challenges as Learning Opportunities**: Instead of seeing difficult math problems as a sign that she wasn't good at math, Kaylie viewed them as opportunities to learn and grow. She reminded herself that every problem she solved, no matter how hard, was helping her improve and get closer to her goal.
2. **Using Affirmations to Boost Confidence**: Kaylie created a set of affirmations that she repeated to herself daily, such as "I am capable of improving my math skills" and "Every effort I make brings me closer to my goal." These affirmations helped her stay focused on her progress and build confidence in her abilities.
3. **Visualizing Success**: Before each test, Kaylie took a few moments to visualize herself doing well. She imagined herself calmly and confidently answering each question, receiving her graded test back with an A, and feeling proud of her hard work. This visualization practice helped reduce her anxiety and reinforced her belief in her ability to succeed.
4. **Practicing Gratitude**: Kaylie kept a gratitude journal where she wrote down three things she was grateful for each day. This practice helped her stay positive and motivated, even on tough days. She found that focusing on the good things in her life helped her maintain a positive outlook and stay committed to her goals.

By maintaining a positive mindset and using these techniques, Kaylie was able to overcome her challenges and achieve her goal of improving her math grade. Her story shows the power of optimism and a growth mindset in achieving success.

Activity: Creating Your Daily Affirmations

Affirmations are a powerful tool for building confidence and maintaining a positive mindset. In this activity, you'll create your own set of daily affirmations to help you stay focused and motivated as you work toward your goals.

Instructions:

1. **Think About Your Goals**: Reflect on your current goals and the qualities you want to reinforce in yourself. What do you need to believe about yourself to achieve these goals?

_____

_____

_____

2. **Write Down Your Affirmations**: Create three to five positive statements that align with your goals and aspirations. Make sure they are specific, positive, and in the present tense. For example:
   o "I am capable of achieving my goals through hard work and determination."
   o "I am confident in my abilities and embrace challenges as opportunities to grow."
   o "I am resilient and can overcome any obstacle that comes my way."

_____

_____

_____

3. **Repeat Your Affirmations Daily**: Set aside a few minutes each day to repeat your affirmations to yourself. You can say them aloud in front of a mirror, write them down in a journal, or even create a reminder on your phone to read them throughout the day.

_____

_____

4. **Reflect on the Impact**: After practicing your affirmations for a week, take a moment to reflect on how they have impacted your mindset and motivation. Write down any changes you've noticed in your confidence or attitude.

_____

_____

_____

Journaling Prompt: How do you feel after repeating your affirmations? Do you notice any changes in your mindset or motivation? Write down your thoughts and feelings in your journal or here.

_____

_____

_____

_____

_____

_____

_____

_____

_____

Reflection: Journaling Your Positive Experiences

Journaling is a powerful tool for cultivating a positive mindset and reflecting on your progress. In this reflection activity, you'll focus on journaling your positive experiences and the lessons you've learned along the way.

Instructions:

1. **Set Aside Time to Journal**: Find a quiet space where you can reflect without distractions. Set aside 10-15 minutes each day to journal your thoughts and experiences.
2. **Reflect on Positive Experiences**: Think about the positive experiences you've had recently, no matter how small. Write down three positive things that happened to you today or this week. These could be successes, kind interactions, or moments of joy.
3. **Explore the Lessons Learned**: For each positive experience, reflect on what you learned and how it has helped you grow. Consider how these experiences have shaped your mindset and moved you closer to your goals.
4. **Set an Intention for Tomorrow**: End your journaling session by setting a positive intention for the next day. This could be something you want to focus on, a quality you want to embody, or a goal you want to achieve.

Journaling Prompt: What positive experiences have you had recently, and what have you learned from them? How have these experiences helped you grow and move closer to your goals?

_____

_____

_____

_____

_____

_____

Maintaining a positive mindset is a powerful tool for achieving your goals and overcoming challenges. By developing a growth mindset, practicing visualization, affirmations, and gratitude, and learning from Kaylie's story, you can build a resilient and optimistic attitude that will support you on your journey to success. Remember, the way you think about yourself and your abilities has a profound impact on your ability to achieve your goals. Stay positive, keep learning, and believe in your potential—you have the power to achieve anything you set your mind to!

Let's continue this journey together and build a positive mindset that empowers you to reach your dreams.

Your mindset plays a huge role in your success. Learn how to stay positive and motivated, even when things get tough. We'll discuss techniques like visualization, affirmations, and journaling to help you keep your eye on the prize and overcome any obstacles that come your way.

Kaylie's Positive Mindset

Kaylie faced many challenges along the way, like difficult math concepts and feeling overwhelmed before big tests. But she maintained a positive mindset by reminding herself of her progress and the reasons she set her goal in the first place. She used visualization techniques, imagining herself confidently solving math problems, and repeated affirmations like, "I am capable of improving my grades."

Activity: Practice Visualization and Affirmations

Follow Kaylie's lead by writing down a few affirmations and spending a few minutes each day visualizing your success.

_____

_____

_____

_____

_____

_____

_____

_____

_____

_____

_____

_____

Chapter 5: Overcoming Obstacles and Staying Resilient

Achieving your goals isn't always a smooth journey. Along the way, you're likely to encounter obstacles that test your determination and resilience. Whether it's a challenging subject in school, a personal setback, or a lack of motivation, these obstacles can sometimes make your goals feel out of reach. However, learning to overcome these challenges is an essential part of personal growth and goal mastery. This chapter will explore common challenges in achieving goals, strategies for overcoming obstacles, and how to build resilience and adaptability. We'll also look at how Kaylie and other teens faced their own challenges and found ways to push through.

Common Challenges in Achieving Goals

No matter how well you plan, you will likely face obstacles on your path to achieving your goals. Understanding some of the common challenges can help you prepare and respond effectively when they arise:

1. **Lack of Motivation**: It's normal to feel excited and motivated when you first set a goal, but as time goes on, that initial excitement can wane. You might start to feel less enthusiastic about the effort required to achieve your goal, leading to procrastination or giving up entirely.
2. **Fear of Failure**: Fear of failing can be paralyzing. You might worry that you're not good enough, that you'll embarrass yourself, or that you'll let others down. This fear can stop you from taking risks or trying new things, which are often necessary steps toward achieving your goals.
3. **Time Management Issues**: Balancing multiple responsibilities, such as school, extracurricular activities, and personal life, can make it difficult to find time for your goals. Poor time management can lead to feeling overwhelmed and stressed, making it hard to stay focused and productive.
4. **Unexpected Setbacks**: Life is unpredictable, and sometimes things happen that are beyond your control, such as illness, family issues, or changes in circumstances. These setbacks can disrupt your plans and make it challenging to stay on track.
5. **Lack of Support**: Sometimes, achieving your goals requires support from others, whether it's encouragement from friends and family or guidance from a mentor. If you lack a strong support system, you might feel isolated and struggle to stay motivated.
6. **Self-Doubt**: Negative self-talk and self-doubt can undermine your confidence and make it hard to believe in your ability to achieve your goals. You might question whether you're capable or deserving of success, which can hinder your progress.

Strategies for Overcoming Obstacles

While obstacles are inevitable, how you respond to them is within your control. Here are some effective strategies for overcoming challenges and staying on course:

1. **Break Down Your Goals into Smaller Steps**: When you're feeling overwhelmed, breaking your goal into smaller, more manageable steps can make it feel less daunting. Focus on completing one step at a time, rather than worrying about the entire journey. This approach helps build momentum and keeps you moving forward.
2. **Revisit Your "Why"**: Remind yourself why you set this goal in the first place. Reflect on what achieving this goal means to you and how it aligns with your values and long-term vision. Reconnecting with your purpose can reignite your motivation and help you push through difficult times.
3. **Develop a Flexible Mindset**: Be open to adjusting your plan if needed. If you encounter a setback, consider alternative ways to reach your goal. Flexibility allows you to adapt to changing circumstances and find new solutions to problems that arise.
4. **Seek Support**: Don't be afraid to ask for help when you need it. Reach out to friends, family, teachers, or mentors who can provide guidance, encouragement, or assistance. Sometimes, just talking about your challenges with someone who understands can make a big difference.
5. **Practice Self-Compassion**: Be kind to yourself when things don't go as planned. Remember that everyone faces setbacks, and it's okay to make mistakes. Treat yourself with the same compassion and understanding you would offer a friend in a similar situation.
6. **Use Positive Affirmations**: Counter negative self-talk with positive affirmations. Remind yourself of your strengths, past successes, and your ability to overcome challenges. Affirmations can help build confidence and reduce self-doubt.
7. **Create a Contingency Plan**: Prepare for potential setbacks by creating a contingency plan. Think about what you'll do if things don't go as expected and how you'll handle obstacles when they arise. Having a plan in place can help reduce anxiety and increase your readiness to face challenges.
8. **Focus on the Progress, Not Perfection**: Recognize that progress, not perfection, is the key to achieving your goals. Celebrate your achievements, no matter how small, and use them as motivation to keep going. Remember, every step forward is a step closer to your goal.

Building Resilience and Adaptability

Resilience is the ability to bounce back from setbacks, adapt to change, and keep going in the face of adversity. It's a crucial quality for anyone who wants to achieve their goals, as it helps you stay focused and motivated, even when things get tough. Here are some ways to build resilience and adaptability:

1. **Embrace a Growth Mindset**: View challenges as opportunities to learn and grow. Understand that setbacks are a natural part of the process and can provide valuable lessons. A growth mindset helps you see difficulties as temporary and surmountable rather than permanent roadblocks.
2. **Practice Mindfulness and Stress Management**: Developing techniques to manage stress, such as mindfulness, meditation, or deep breathing exercises, can help you stay calm and focused when faced with challenges. Mindfulness encourages you to stay present and approach difficulties with a clear, open mind.
3. **Cultivate Patience and Persistence**: Understand that achieving your goals takes time and effort. Be patient with yourself and stay committed, even when progress is slow. Persistence is key to overcoming obstacles and reaching your goals, so keep pushing forward, even when it's challenging.
4. **Learn from Your Experiences**: Reflect on past challenges and what you learned from them. Use these insights to inform your future actions and improve your approach to obstacles. Learning from experience helps you become more adaptable and better prepared to handle future setbacks.
5. **Maintain a Support Network**: Surround yourself with supportive people who believe in you and your goals. A strong support network can provide encouragement, advice, and a sense of community, helping you stay resilient in the face of adversity.
6. **Set Realistic Expectations**: Understand that not everything will go perfectly according to plan. Be prepared for ups and downs and set realistic expectations for yourself. This mindset helps you stay flexible and open to change, making it easier to adapt when things don't go as expected.

Kaylie's Story: How She Overcame Setbacks

Kaylie's journey to improving her math grade wasn't without its challenges. Along the way, she faced several setbacks that tested her resolve and determination. However, by staying positive, flexible, and resilient, Kaylie was able to overcome these obstacles and achieve her goal.

Challenges Kaylie Faced:

1. **Difficult Math Concepts**: Kaylie struggled with some of the more challenging math concepts covered in her class. Despite her efforts, she sometimes felt overwhelmed and unsure of how to proceed.
2. **Time Constraints**: Balancing her math studies with other schoolwork and extracurricular activities proved challenging. Kaylie often found it difficult to manage her time effectively, leading to stress and frustration.
3. **Self-Doubt**: At times, Kaylie doubted her ability to improve her math grade. She worried that she wasn't smart enough or that she wouldn't be able to meet her goal.

Strategies Kaylie Used to Overcome These Setbacks:

1. **Seeking Help**: When faced with difficult math concepts, Kaylie reached out for help. She asked her teacher for extra explanations and attended tutoring sessions to get additional support. By seeking help, she was able to gain a better understanding of the material and build her confidence.
2. **Creating a Flexible Study Schedule**: To address her time management challenges, Kaylie created a flexible study schedule that allowed her to balance her math studies with other commitments. She allocated specific times each day for studying and adjusted her schedule as needed to accommodate changes in her routine.
3. **Using Positive Self-Talk and Affirmations**: When self-doubt crept in, Kaylie countered it with positive self-talk and affirmations. She reminded herself of her past successes and her ability to learn and improve. This practice helped her stay focused on her progress and maintain a positive mindset.
4. **Celebrating Small Wins**: Kaylie celebrated each small victory along the way, whether it was understanding a difficult concept or getting a good grade on a quiz. These celebrations kept her motivated and reinforced her belief in her ability to achieve her goal.

Kaylie's story demonstrates the importance of resilience, flexibility, and a positive mindset in overcoming obstacles. By using these strategies, she was able to push through her challenges and achieve her goal of improving her math grade.

Case Studies: Real-Life Examples of Teens Facing and Overcoming Challenges

Let's look at a few more real-life examples of teens who faced challenges and found ways to overcome them. These stories highlight the power of perseverance, creativity, and resilience in achieving goals.

Case Study 1: Jamie's Journey to the Soccer Team Jamie was determined to make the school soccer team, but during tryouts, she struggled to keep up with the more experienced players. She felt discouraged and worried she wouldn't make the team. Instead of giving up, Jamie decided to create a plan to improve her skills. She practiced every day after school, focusing on her weaker areas and seeking advice from her coach. Jamie also joined a local soccer clinic to get additional training. By the time the final tryouts came around, Jamie's skills had improved significantly, and she made the team. Jamie's story shows that with determination and a willingness to seek help, you can overcome obstacles and achieve your goals.

Case Study 2: Emily's Battle with Stage Fright Emily had always dreamed of performing in her school's talent show, but she struggled with severe stage fright. The thought of performing in front of a large audience made her feel anxious and afraid. Determined to conquer her fear, Emily decided to take small steps toward her goal. She started by performing in front of a few friends and gradually increased the size of her audience. Emily also practiced visualization and deep breathing techniques to calm her nerves. By the time the talent show arrived, Emily felt more confident and performed beautifully, earning a standing ovation. Emily's story demonstrates the power of gradual exposure and positive thinking in overcoming fears.

Case Study 3: Ryan's Academic Comeback Ryan had always been a good student, but during his junior year, he struggled with a particularly tough physics class. After failing the first few tests, Ryan felt discouraged and considered dropping the class. However, he decided to stick with it and develop a new approach to studying. Ryan joined a study group, sought extra help from his teacher, and created a detailed study schedule to keep himself on track. He also used positive affirmations to boost his confidence and stay motivated. By the end of the semester, Ryan had improved his grade significantly and passed the class with a B. Ryan's story highlights the importance of persistence, planning, and positive self-talk in overcoming academic challenges.

Worksheet: Identifying Your Obstacles and Strategies

This worksheet will help you identify potential obstacles you might face in achieving your goals and develop strategies to overcome them.

1. **Identify Potential Obstacles**:

What challenges might you face on your journey to achieving your goals? List at least three potential obstacles.

_____

_____

_____

2. **Develop Strategies for Overcoming Each Obstacle**:

For each obstacle you listed, brainstorm strategies for overcoming it. Think about what resources or support you might need and how you can approach the challenge with a positive mindset.
   - Obstacle 1:
     - Strategy: _____
   - Obstacle 2:
     - Strategy: _____
   - Obstacle 3:
     - Strategy: _____

3. **Create a Contingency Plan**:

How will you adjust your plan if things don't go as expected? What steps will you take to stay on track despite setbacks?

_____

_____

_____

4. **Reflect on Past Challenges**:

Think about a challenge you've faced in the past and how you overcame it. What strategies did you use? How can you apply those strategies to your current goals?

_____

Use this worksheet to prepare for potential obstacles and develop a plan to overcome them. Remember, challenges are a natural part of the journey, and by building resilience and adaptability, you can stay focused and achieve your goals.

Overcoming obstacles is an essential part of the goal-setting process. By understanding common challenges, developing effective strategies, and building resilience, you can stay on track and achieve your goals, no matter what difficulties you face. Remember, every obstacle is an opportunity to learn and grow. With determination, flexibility, and a positive mindset, you can overcome any challenge and reach your dreams. Let's continue this journey together, building resilience and staying strong as you work toward your goals!

Chapter 6: Time Management for Teen

Time is one of the most valuable resources you have, and learning how to manage it effectively can make a huge difference in achieving your goals. As a teen, you juggle schoolwork, extracurricular activities, social life, family responsibilities, and perhaps even a part-time job. It's easy to feel overwhelmed and struggle to find enough time to do everything you need to do. That's why mastering time management is so important. This chapter will explore the importance of time management, offer techniques for managing your time effectively, and show you how to use digital tools to stay organized. We'll also look at Kaylie's time management strategy and provide activities and worksheets to help you create and track your own time management plan.

The Importance of Time Management

Effective time management is crucial for several reasons:

1. **Maximizes Productivity**: By managing your time well, you can get more done in less time. This allows you to focus on what's most important, whether it's studying for a test, practicing for a sports event, or spending quality time with friends and family. Good time management helps you prioritize tasks, eliminate procrastination, and ensure that you are working efficiently.
2. **Reduces Stress**: When you have a clear plan for how to use your time, you're less likely to feel overwhelmed by your responsibilities. Time management helps you break down large tasks into smaller, more manageable steps, making it easier to stay on top of everything and avoid last-minute stress.
3. **Improves Focus and Concentration**: When you manage your time effectively, you can dedicate specific blocks of time to different tasks without distractions. This allows you to fully focus on the task at hand, which can improve the quality of your work and help you complete tasks more quickly.
4. **Increases Opportunities for Personal Growth**: Good time management allows you to make time for personal interests, hobbies, and self-care, which are essential for personal growth and well-being. By balancing your responsibilities with your passions, you create a more fulfilling and well-rounded life.
5. **Helps Achieve Goals**: Time management is key to achieving both short-term and long-term goals. By allocating time to work on your goals consistently, you make steady progress and avoid feeling stuck or unmotivated. Effective time management ensures that you are always moving forward toward your desired outcomes.

Techniques for Effective Time Management

Managing your time effectively requires planning, discipline, and the right strategies. Here are some techniques to help you make the most of your time:

1. **Prioritize Your Tasks**: Start by making a list of all the tasks you need to complete. Then, prioritize them based on their importance and urgency. Focus on completing high-priority tasks first and tackle less important tasks afterward. This helps you make the most of your time and ensures that you're working on what matters most.
   - **The Eisenhower Matrix**: This is a useful tool for prioritizing tasks. Divide your tasks into four categories:
     - **Urgent and Important**: Tasks that need immediate attention (e.g., studying for an upcoming test).
     - **Important but Not Urgent**: Tasks that are important but can be scheduled for later (e.g., working on a long-term project).
     - **Urgent but Not Important**: Tasks that require immediate action but are not crucial (e.g., replying to a non-urgent message).
     - **Not Urgent and Not Important**: Tasks that can be eliminated or postponed (e.g., browsing social media).
2. **Use a To-Do List**: Writing down your tasks and goals for the day can help you stay organized and focused. A to-do list provides a clear overview of what needs to be done and gives you a sense of accomplishment as you check off completed tasks. Keep your to-do list realistic and manageable by limiting it to a few key tasks each day.
3. **Break Tasks into Smaller Steps**: Large tasks can feel overwhelming, leading to procrastination. Break them down into smaller, more manageable steps. For example, instead of writing "study for math test" on your to-do list, break it down into steps like "review math notes," "complete practice problems," and "quiz yourself on key concepts." This makes the task feel less daunting and easier to start.
4. **Set Specific Time Blocks for Tasks**: Allocate specific time blocks in your schedule for different tasks. For example, set aside time for studying, attending extracurricular activities, and relaxing. This helps create a routine and ensures that you're dedicating enough time to each area of your life. Be sure to include short breaks to rest and recharge.
5. **Avoid Multitasking**: While it may seem like multitasking helps you get more done, it can actually reduce productivity and the quality of your work. Focus on one task at a time, giving it your full attention, and then move on to the next task. This approach improves efficiency and reduces errors.
6. **Set Deadlines for Yourself**: Deadlines create a sense of urgency and help prevent procrastination. Set realistic deadlines for each task and stick to them. This will keep you on track and ensure that you're making steady progress toward your goals.
7. **Review and Reflect**: At the end of each day or week, review what you've accomplished and reflect on what went well and what could be improved. Use this reflection to adjust your time management strategies as needed and to plan for the week ahead. Regular reflection helps you stay organized and continually improve your time management skills.

Using Digital Tools: Calendars, Reminders, and Productivity Apps

In today's digital age, there are many tools available to help you manage your time effectively. Here's how to make the most of digital tools:

1. **Digital Calendars**: Use a digital calendar, such as Google Calendar or Apple Calendar, to schedule your tasks, classes, extracurricular activities, and personal time. Color-code different types of activities to make your calendar easy to read and understand at a glance. Set reminders for important deadlines and events to stay on track.

2. **Reminders**: Use the reminder feature on your phone or computer to set alerts for important tasks and deadlines. Reminders can help you stay organized and ensure you don't forget important commitments. You can also use reminders for daily habits, like "drink water" or "stretch," to maintain a healthy routine.

3. **Productivity Apps**: There are many productivity apps designed to help you stay focused and manage your time effectively. Apps like Todoist, Notion, and Microsoft To Do allow you to create to-do lists, set deadlines, and track your progress. Find an app that works best for you and integrate it into your daily routine.

4. **Time Tracking Apps**: Apps like RescueTime or Toggl can help you track how much time you spend on different activities throughout the day. This information can help you identify time-wasting habits and adjust your schedule to be more productive.

5. **Focus Apps**: Focus apps like Forest or Focus@Will provide a structured environment for focused work. Forest, for example, encourages you to stay off your phone by growing a virtual tree while you focus on a task. If you use your phone during the focus period, your tree dies. Focus@Will offers background music designed to improve concentration and productivity.

6. **Note-Taking Apps**: Apps like Evernote or OneNote can help you keep track of ideas, notes, and reminders all in one place. Use these apps to jot down important information, make study guides, or brainstorm ideas for projects. Having everything in one digital location makes it easy to stay organized and quickly access what you need.

7. **Digital Planners**: If you prefer a planner format but want the benefits of digital tools, consider using a digital planner. These planners often come with templates for daily, weekly, and monthly planning, habit tracking, and goal setting. They can be used on tablets with styluses or on your computer, combining the best of both digital and traditional planning.

8. **Practice the Pomodoro Technique**: This technique involves working in focused bursts of 25 minutes, followed by a short 5-minute break. After four work periods, take a longer break of 15-30 minutes. This method helps maintain concentration and prevent burnout, making it easier to stay productive throughout the day.

By using digital tools, you can streamline your time management processes and make it easier to stay organized and focused.

Kaylie's Time Management Strategy

Kaylie knew that improving her math grade would require a solid time management strategy. With a busy schedule that included schoolwork, extracurricular activities, and family responsibilities, she needed to find a way to balance everything while still dedicating enough time to her studies.

Here's how Kaylie managed her time effectively:

1. **Creating a Weekly Schedule**: Kaylie started by creating a weekly schedule that outlined all her commitments, including school, homework, tutoring sessions, and extracurricular activities. She used a digital calendar to block out specific times for each task and color-coded them for easy reference. This visual overview helped her see where her time was going and ensured that she was allocating enough time to each area of her life.
2. **Setting Priorities**: Kaylie prioritized her tasks based on their importance and deadlines. She made sure to focus on her most critical tasks first, such as studying for an upcoming math test or completing a major project. By tackling her high-priority tasks early in the day, she felt more accomplished and less stressed about her remaining responsibilities.
3. **Using the Pomodoro Technique**: To stay focused and avoid burnout, Kaylie used the Pomodoro Technique. She set a timer for 25 minutes and focused solely on one task during that time. After 25 minutes, she took a 5-minute break to stretch, grab a snack, or relax. This method helped her stay productive and maintain her concentration throughout her study sessions.
4. **Incorporating Short Breaks**: Kaylie recognized the importance of taking breaks to recharge. She scheduled short breaks between study sessions and longer breaks for meals or relaxation. These breaks helped her stay refreshed and prevented fatigue, allowing her to study more effectively over time.
5. **Tracking Progress and Adjusting**: Each week, Kaylie reviewed her progress and adjusted her schedule as needed. If she noticed that she wasn't spending enough time on a particular subject or activity, she made changes to ensure a better balance. This regular reflection helped her stay on track and make continuous improvements to her time management strategy.

6. **Leveraging Digital Tools**: Kaylie used digital tools like Google Calendar for scheduling and Todoist for managing her to-do lists. She set reminders for important deadlines and used focus apps to minimize distractions while studying. These tools helped her stay organized and made it easier to manage her time effectively.

By implementing these strategies, Kaylie was able to balance her responsibilities and make steady progress toward her goal of improving her math grade. Her time management skills not only helped her achieve her academic goals but also allowed her to maintain a healthy and balanced lifestyle.

Activity: Create Your Weekly Time Management Plan

Creating a weekly time management plan can help you organize your schedule, prioritize your tasks, and ensure you're making time for what matters most. Follow these steps to create your plan:

Instructions:

1. **List Your Weekly Commitments**: Write down all of your weekly commitments, including school, extracurricular activities, chores, and personal time. Be as specific as possible to get a clear picture of your week.
2. **Prioritize Your Tasks**: Identify which tasks are most important and urgent. These should be your top priorities for the week. Consider using the Eisenhower Matrix to help with prioritization.
3. **Create a Time Block Schedule**: Use a blank weekly calendar to create time blocks for each of your commitments. Color-code different types of activities to make your schedule easy to read.
4. **Include Breaks and Personal Time**: Make sure to include time for breaks, relaxation, and self-care. It's important to maintain a balanced schedule that supports both productivity and well-being.
5. **Set Goals for Each Time Block**: For each time block, set a specific goal or task to complete. This will help you stay focused and ensure you're making progress toward your goals.
6. **Review and Adjust as Needed**: At the end of the week, review your schedule to see what worked well and what didn't. Adjust as needed to improve your time management strategy for the following week.

Journaling Prompt: Reflect on your time management plan for the week. What went well? What could be improved? How did your plan help you stay organized and focused on your goals?

_____

_____

_____

_____

_____

_____

_____

_____

_____

_____

_____

_____

_____

_____

_____

_____

_____

_____

_____

_____

_____

_____

_____

_____

_____

_____

_____

_____

_____

Worksheet: Tracking Your Time and Adjusting Your Schedule

Tracking your time can help you understand how you're spending your days and identify areas for improvement. Use this worksheet to track your time and adjust your schedule as needed.

1. Track Your Time for One Week:

- Use a blank weekly calendar or a time-tracking app to record how you spend your time each day. Be honest and detailed, including everything from studying and attending classes to socializing and relaxing.

2. Reflect on Your Time Usage:

- At the end of the week, review your time tracking. Are there any patterns or habits that stand out? Are you spending too much time on certain activities and not enough on others?
- What surprised you about how you spent your time? What did you do well, and where could you improve?

3. Identify Time-Wasting Habits:

- Look for any time-wasting habits that might be hindering your productivity. This could include excessive time on social media, procrastination, or unnecessary multitasking.
- Write down two or three time-wasting habits you'd like to change.

4. Develop a Plan to Adjust Your Schedule:

- Based on your reflection, create a plan to adjust your schedule. Consider how you can allocate more time to high-priority tasks and reduce time spent on low-priority activities.
- Make a list of changes you'd like to implement for the upcoming week.

5. Set New Goals for Time Management:

- What are your goals for improving your time management next week? Be specific about what you want to achieve and how you'll measure your progress.

Journaling Prompt: After adjusting your schedule and setting new goals, write about how these changes are helping you stay on track and achieve your goals. What impact do you notice in your productivity and stress levels?

_____

_____

_____

_____

_____

_____

_____

_____

_____

_____

_____

_____

_____

_____

_____

_____

_____

_____

Effective time management is a crucial skill that can help you balance your responsibilities, reduce stress, and achieve your goals. By learning how to prioritize tasks, use digital tools, and create a structured schedule, you can make the most of your time and set yourself up for success. Remember, time management is a skill that takes practice, so be patient with yourself and keep adjusting as needed. With the right strategies and mindset, you can take control of your time and make steady progress toward your dreams. Let's continue this journey together, mastering time management and achieving your goals!

Chapter 7: Building Your Support Squad

Achieving your goals isn't something you have to do alone. In fact, having a strong support system can make all the difference in helping you stay motivated, overcome obstacles, and celebrate your successes. Your support squad includes the people who encourage you, guide you, and believe in your potential. In this chapter, we'll explore why you need a support system, how to identify the people in your life who can be part of your support squad, and how to ask for help and offer support to others. We'll also take a closer look at Kaylie's support network and provide activities and worksheets to help you build and strengthen your own support system.

Why You Need a Support System

A support system is a group of people who provide emotional, social, and practical support as you work toward your goals. Here's why having a support system is so important:

1. **Emotional Encouragement**: Pursuing your goals can be challenging and sometimes lonely. Having people who believe in you and offer encouragement can boost your confidence and help you stay motivated, especially during tough times. Emotional support helps you feel valued, understood, and capable of achieving your dreams.
2. **Accountability**: A strong support system can hold you accountable for your commitments. When others are aware of your goals and progress, you're more likely to stay committed and follow through. Accountability partners can help you stay focused, remind you of your purpose, and encourage you to keep going, even when you feel like giving up.
3. **Advice and Guidance**: Your support squad can provide valuable advice and guidance based on their own experiences and expertise. They can offer insights, share resources, and help you navigate challenges more effectively. Whether it's a mentor guiding you through a difficult decision or a friend sharing study tips, having access to diverse perspectives can enhance your ability to achieve your goals.
4. **Practical Support**: Sometimes, achieving your goals requires more than just emotional encouragement; you may also need practical help. This could include a friend helping you study for a test, a family member assisting with a project, or a mentor providing feedback on your work. Practical support helps lighten the load and makes it easier to manage your responsibilities.
5. **Celebrating Success**: Achieving a goal is a significant accomplishment, and celebrating your successes with others can make the experience even more rewarding. Your support squad will be there to cheer you on and celebrate your victories, big or small. Sharing these moments with others can reinforce your motivation and inspire you to set and achieve new goals.

6. **Building Resilience**: A strong support system can help you build resilience by providing encouragement and perspective when you face setbacks. They can help you see challenges as opportunities for growth and remind you of your strengths and abilities. This support helps you stay positive and focused, even when things don't go as planned.

Identifying Your Support Squad: Friends, Family, Mentors, and Coaches

Your support squad can be made up of a variety of people, each bringing unique strengths and perspectives to the table. Here's how to identify the different types of support you may have in your life:

1. **Friends**: Friends are often the first people we turn to for support. They know us well, understand our struggles, and can provide both emotional encouragement and practical help. Think about which friends you can rely on to be positive, supportive, and honest. These are the friends who will cheer you on, offer a listening ear, and stand by you through thick and thin.
2. **Family**: Family members can provide a strong foundation of support, especially during challenging times. Whether it's parents, siblings, or extended family, these individuals often have a vested interest in your success and can offer valuable advice and assistance. Consider which family members you feel comfortable turning to for guidance and support.
3. **Mentors**: Mentors are individuals with experience and knowledge in a specific area who can provide guidance, advice, and inspiration. They can be teachers, coaches, community leaders, or professionals in a field you're interested in. A mentor can help you set goals, navigate challenges, and provide valuable feedback to help you grow and develop.
4. **Coaches**: Coaches, whether in sports, academics, or personal development, are there to help you improve and achieve your goals. They provide structured guidance, encouragement, and constructive feedback to help you reach your full potential. A coach's role is to challenge you, support your growth, and help you stay on track.
5. **Classmates and Peers**: Your classmates and peers can also be an important part of your support squad. They're often working toward similar goals and can provide mutual support, share resources, and offer encouragement. Collaborating with peers on study groups, projects, or extracurricular activities can create a strong sense of camaraderie and shared purpose.
6. **Online Communities**: In today's digital age, support can also come from online communities and social networks. There are countless forums, groups, and platforms where people with similar interests or goals connect to offer support, share experiences, and provide advice. Online communities can be a great source of inspiration and motivation, especially if you're looking for support beyond your immediate circle.

Identifying your support squad involves recognizing the people in your life who are willing to help you, who share your values, and who believe in your potential. Take some time to think about who these individuals are and how they can contribute to your journey.

How to Ask for Help and Offer Support to Others

Asking for help can sometimes feel uncomfortable, but it's an essential part of building a strong support system. Here are some tips for asking for help and offering support to others:

1. Be Clear About Your Needs: When asking for help, be specific about what you need. Whether it's advice, encouragement, or practical assistance, being clear about your request makes it easier for others to offer the right kind of support. For example, instead of saying, "I need help with my homework," you might say, "Can you help me review my math problems for an hour this evening?"

2. Choose the Right Time and Place: Approach people when they're likely to be receptive to your request. Choose a time when they're not busy or stressed and a place where you can have a private conversation if needed. This shows respect for their time and increases the likelihood that they'll be willing to help.

3. Be Honest and Authentic: Share your reasons for needing help and why it's important to you. Being honest about your struggles and aspirations can build trust and make others more willing to support you. Remember, everyone needs help sometimes, and asking for it is a sign of strength, not weakness.

4. Show Appreciation: Always express gratitude to those who offer their support. Whether it's a simple thank you or a heartfelt note, showing appreciation reinforces your relationship and encourages people to continue supporting you in the future. Acknowledge their help and let them know how much it means to you.

5. Offer Support in Return: Building a strong support system is a two-way street. Be willing to offer your support to others, whether it's listening to a friend, providing advice, or helping with a project. When you show that you're there for others, they're more likely to be there for you in return.

6. Be Respectful of Boundaries: Understand that everyone has their own limits and boundaries. If someone is unable or unwilling to help, respect their decision without taking it personally. Focus on finding support from other members of your squad and remain open to new connections.

Kaylie's Support Network: Who Helped Her and How

Kaylie's journey to improving her math grade was supported by a strong network of individuals who believed in her potential and provided guidance, encouragement, and practical assistance. Here's a closer look at Kaylie's support network and how each member contributed to her success:

1. **Her Math Teacher**: Kaylie's math teacher played a significant role in her journey. Recognizing her determination, the teacher offered extra help after class and provided additional resources for practice. The teacher's willingness to go the extra mile made a big difference in Kaylie's understanding of the material and her confidence in her abilities.
2. **Her Parents**: Kaylie's parents were a constant source of encouragement. They provided a quiet space for her to study, helped her manage her time effectively, and offered emotional support when she felt discouraged. They reminded her of her strengths and reinforced the importance of perseverance, helping her stay motivated throughout her journey.
3. **Her Tutor**: To get additional support, Kaylie worked with a tutor who specialized in math. The tutor provided personalized instruction, explained difficult concepts in a way that made sense to Kaylie, and helped her develop effective study strategies. The one-on-one attention and tailored guidance helped Kaylie overcome her challenges and build confidence in her math skills.
4. **Her Best Friend**: Kaylie's best friend was a crucial part of her support squad. They studied together, encouraged each other, and celebrated each other's successes. Her friend provided emotional support, listened to her frustrations, and cheered her on, making the journey more enjoyable and less stressful.
5. **Her Study Group**: Kaylie also joined a study group with other students who were working to improve their math grades. The group met regularly to review material, share study tips, and quiz each other on key concepts. The collaborative environment helped Kaylie stay engaged and motivated, and she benefited from the diverse perspectives and strategies shared within the group.

Kaylie's support network was instrumental in her success. Each member played a unique role in helping her achieve her goal, demonstrating the power of a strong, diverse support system.

Reflection Activity: Who is in Your Support Squad?

Reflecting on who is in your support squad can help you appreciate the people who are already supporting you and identify areas where you might need additional support.

Instructions:

1. **List Your Current Support Squad**: Write down the names of people who currently support you in your goals. Include friends, family, mentors, coaches, and anyone else who plays a positive role in your life.

_____

_____

_____

2. **Identify Their Roles**: Next to each name, write down how they support you. Are they a source of emotional encouragement? Do they provide practical help or advice? Understanding the different roles people play can help you recognize the strengths of your support squad.

_____

_____

_____

3. **Consider Who Else Could Be Part of Your Squad**: Think about people you know who aren't currently part of your support squad but could be. This might include teachers, classmates, community leaders, or people in online communities. How might they be able to support you in achieving your goals?

_____

_____

_____

4. **Reflect on How You Can Strengthen Your Support Network**: Consider ways you can strengthen your support network by building deeper connections, asking for help when needed, and offering your support to others. Write down a few actions you can take to build and strengthen your support squad.

_____

_____

_____

Journaling Prompt: Reflect on the people in your support squad and how they contribute to your goals. How do you feel about the support you currently have? Are there any gaps you'd like to fill, or relationships you'd like to strengthen?

_____

_____

_____

_____

_____

_____

_____

_____

_____

_____

_____

_____

_____

_____

_____

_____

_____

_____

Worksheet: Building and Strengthening Your Support Network

Building and maintaining a strong support network is essential for achieving your goals. Use this worksheet to identify ways to build and strengthen your support squad.

1. Identify Key Support Roles:

- List the different roles you need in your support squad (e.g., emotional support, accountability partner, mentor, coach, study buddy).

- Write down the names of people who currently fill these roles or who you think could fill these roles.

_____

_____

_____

_____

_____

2. Plan to Strengthen Existing Relationships:

- For each person in your support squad, write down one way you can strengthen your relationship with them (e.g., spending more time together, offering help, communicating more openly).

_____

_____

_____

_____

_____

3. Identify Gaps in Your Support Network:

- Are there any roles in your support network that aren't currently filled? Write down the roles and consider who might be able to fill them.

_____

_____

_____

4. Take Action to Build New Connections:

- Identify at least two people you'd like to build a stronger connection with. Write down specific actions you can take to reach out to them and build a supportive relationship (e.g., asking for advice, inviting them to collaborate on a project, joining a club or group they're involved in).

_____

_____

_____

5. Reflect on How You Can Offer Support:

- Building a strong support network isn't just about receiving support—it's also about giving it. Write down three ways you can offer support to others in your network (e.g., offering to help with a task, being a good listener, providing encouragement).

_____

_____

_____

Journaling Prompt: Reflect on the actions you've taken to build and strengthen your support network. How has your support squad changed or grown? How do you feel about the support you're giving and receiving?

_____

_____

_____

_____

_____

_____

_____

_____

_____

_____

_____

_____

_____

_____

_____

_____

_____

_____

_____

_____

_____

_____

_____

_____

Building a strong support squad is crucial for achieving your goals and overcoming challenges. By identifying the people who can support you, learning how to ask for help, and offering support to others, you can create a network of positive, encouraging relationships that help you stay motivated and resilient. Remember, achieving your goals is a team effort, and you don't have to do it alone. Let's continue this journey together, building a strong support system that empowers you to reach your dreams!

Chapter 8: Celebrating Success and Reflecting on Your Journey

Congratulations! You've worked hard, stayed committed, and made progress toward your goals. That's no small feat! Whether you've achieved a major milestone or taken one small step forward, every bit of progress matters. But what's next? In this chapter, we'll dive into why celebrating your wins is just as important as achieving them and how reflecting on your journey can unlock even greater success in the future.

Why Celebrate Success?

When you celebrate your successes, you're sending yourself a powerful message: "I'm proud of what I've accomplished." This boost of confidence reinforces positive habits, keeps you motivated, and reminds you of your ability to overcome challenges.

Here's why celebrating matters:

1. **Builds Momentum**: Every celebration energizes you to keep going. It's like refueling your car for the next stretch of the journey.
2. **Boosts Self-Esteem**: Recognizing your hard work helps you feel proud of your abilities and growth.
3. **Creates Positive Memories**: Celebrations remind you of the joy in achieving something meaningful, making the process even more rewarding.
4. **Encourages Gratitude**: It's an opportunity to be thankful for the people and circumstances that helped you succeed.

How to Celebrate Meaningfully

Celebration doesn't have to be extravagant. What matters most is that it feels special to you. Here are some meaningful ways to celebrate:

- **Personal Rewards**: Treat yourself to something you enjoy, like an afternoon at your favorite park, a fun DIY project, or a new book.
- **Share Your Win**: Talk to a friend, family member, or mentor about your achievement. Their excitement will amplify your own.
- **Creative Celebrations**: Make a playlist of songs that represent your success, bake a treat to enjoy, or create a visual reminder like a poster or vision board update.
- **Physical Celebrations**: Dance around your room, take a celebratory walk, or do something active that makes you feel good.

- **"Thank You" Moments**: Show gratitude to the people who supported you by writing thank-you notes or telling them how much their help meant to you.

Example: After Kaylie improved her math grade, she treated herself to a cozy movie night with her favorite snacks. She also shared the news with her study group, and they all celebrated together with a pizza party.

Celebrating Small Wins

Sometimes we focus so much on the "big goal" that we overlook the smaller steps that get us there. But every small win is a step closer to your dreams—and that deserves recognition.

How to Celebrate Small Wins:

1. **Daily Acknowledgment**: Write one thing you did well each day in a journal.
2. **Mini Rewards**: Treat yourself to something small, like a piece of chocolate or 10 extra minutes of free time.
3. **Reflection Time**: Take a moment to think about what this step means in the bigger picture of your goal.

Activity: Write down five small wins you've achieved this week. Next to each, write how you celebrated or plan to celebrate.

_____

_____

_____

_____

_____

_____

_____

The Power of Reflection

Reflection is your secret weapon for personal growth. It's like looking in a mirror—not just to see where you are but to understand how you got there and where you want to go next.

Why Reflection is Important:

- **Learn From Experience**: Understand what worked and what didn't so you can improve.
- **Build Self-Awareness**: Recognize your strengths and areas for growth.
- **Celebrate Growth**: Reflection helps you see how far you've come, even when the journey felt slow or difficult.
- **Set Better Goals**: Use what you've learned to set new, more focused goals.

How to Reflect Effectively

Here's a simple process for reflecting on your progress:

1. **Ask Yourself These Questions**:
    - What am I most proud of accomplishing?
    - What challenges did I face, and how did I overcome them?
    - What did I learn about myself during this journey?
    - What could I do differently next time?
2. **Use a Reflection Journal**: Dedicate a notebook or digital file to journaling about your progress. Write about your successes, lessons, and feelings.
3. **Share Your Reflections**: Talk about your journey with a mentor, teacher, or trusted friend. Sometimes, hearing their perspective can give you new insights.
4. **Celebrate Growth**: Reflect on how much you've grown since you started. Think about the skills you've gained, the fears you've overcome, and the habits you've built.

Example: After finishing her science project, Kaylie reflected on her experience. She realized that breaking the project into smaller tasks helped her stay organized. She also learned that asking for feedback from her teacher improved her final work.

Activity: Write a Letter to Your Future Self

Writing to your future self is a powerful way to reflect on your journey and set intentions for the road ahead. Imagine opening this letter in a year and seeing how far you've come.

Instructions:

1. **Start with the Present**: Write about your current goals, dreams, and challenges.
2. **Offer Encouragement**: Remind your future self to stay strong, motivated, and proud.
3. **Dream Big**: Write about what you hope your future self has achieved.

Example:

Dear Future Me,

You've worked so hard to get here, and I hope you're proud of yourself. Right now, I'm learning to manage my time and stay confident in my abilities. I know you've overcome challenges and grown even stronger. Keep setting goals, celebrating your wins, and believing in your dreams. You've got this!

_____

_____

_____

_____

_____

_____

_____

_____

_____

_____

_____

_____

Activity: Plan Your Next Celebration

Think about a goal you're currently working toward. How will you celebrate once you achieve it? Be creative and make it meaningful.

Worksheet Example:
Goal: Improve my running time for the track meet.
Celebration: Go to the park for a picnic with my family and take fun photos to remember the moment.

_____

_____

_____

_____

_____

_____

_____

_____

_____

_____

_____

_____

_____

_____

_____

_____

_____

Final Thoughts on Celebrating and Reflecting

Celebrating success and reflecting on your journey are not just nice-to-haves—they're essential for long-term growth and happiness. They remind you of your potential, give you the confidence to keep going, and help you set even bigger goals for the future.

You've already achieved so much—so take a moment to appreciate yourself. You're learning, growing, and becoming the amazing person you're meant to be. Let each success, small or big, be a step toward your brightest future.

Reflection Journal:

- What is one success you're most proud of, and why?
- How has reflection helped you grow?
- What's one way you plan to celebrate your next win?

_____

_____

_____

_____

_____

_____

_____

_____

_____

_____

_____

_____

Chapter 9: Goal Setting for Different Areas of Your Life

Setting goals isn't just about academics or one specific area of your life—it's about creating a well-rounded plan that helps you grow in multiple aspects. Whether it's excelling in school, pursuing your passions in extracurricular activities, or focusing on personal development, setting goals in different areas ensures you're continuously improving and achieving balance. In this chapter, we'll explore how to set goals for school and academics, extracurricular activities and hobbies, and personal development and well-being. We'll also learn from Kaylie's experience in balancing her diverse goals and provide a worksheet to help you create goals for different areas of your life.

Setting Goals for School and Academics

Academic success is a common area where many teens set goals. Whether it's improving grades, developing better study habits, or mastering a challenging subject, setting clear, achievable academic goals can help you stay focused and motivated.

1. **Identify Your Academic Priorities**: Start by identifying what's most important to you in your academic life. Are there specific subjects you want to excel in, or skills you want to develop? Are you aiming for a particular GPA, or are you preparing for college entrance exams? Understanding your priorities will help you set goals that align with your long-term academic aspirations.
2. **Set Specific, Measurable Goals**: When setting academic goals, be as specific as possible. Instead of setting a vague goal like "do better in math," set a specific, measurable goal such as "raise my math grade from a B to an A by the end of the semester." This gives you a clear target to aim for and makes it easier to track your progress.
3. **Develop a Study Plan**: Once you've set your academic goals, create a study plan that outlines the steps you need to take to achieve them. This might include setting aside specific times for studying each day, seeking help from teachers or tutors, joining study groups, or using additional resources like online tutorials.
4. **Stay Organized**: Use tools like planners, calendars, or apps to keep track of assignments, deadlines, and study sessions. Staying organized helps you manage your time effectively and ensures you're consistently working toward your academic goals.
5. **Celebrate Milestones**: Recognize and celebrate your progress along the way. Whether it's acing a test, completing a challenging project, or mastering a difficult concept, celebrating these milestones can boost your motivation and keep you focused on your larger goals

Setting Goals for Extracurricular Activities and Hobbies

Extracurricular activities and hobbies play a crucial role in personal growth and development. They allow you to explore your interests, build new skills, and develop relationships outside of the classroom. Here's how to set effective goals for your extracurricular activities and hobbies:

1. **Identify Your Interests and Passions**: Start by thinking about what activities or hobbies you're passionate about. Whether it's playing a sport, participating in a club, learning an instrument, or engaging in a creative hobby like writing or drawing, identifying your interests will help you set meaningful goals.
2. **Set Goals that Challenge You**: Aim to set goals that push you out of your comfort zone and encourage you to grow. For example, if you're in a debate club, you might set a goal to become a more confident public speaker. If you're on a sports team, your goal might be to improve a specific skill or lead your team in a particular area.
3. **Balance Extracurriculars with Academics**: It's important to find a balance between your extracurricular activities and academic responsibilities. Set goals that allow you to pursue your passions without compromising your academic performance. This might involve managing your time carefully, prioritizing your activities, or making adjustments to your schedule as needed.
4. **Incorporate Skill Development**: Think about how your extracurricular activities can help you develop new skills. For example, participating in a drama club can improve your public speaking and teamwork skills, while learning an instrument can enhance your discipline and focus. Set goals that focus on skill development as well as performance outcomes.
5. **Reflect on Your Progress**: Regularly reflect on your progress and consider what you've learned from your extracurricular activities. Are you enjoying the activity? Are you growing and developing new skills? Use these reflections to adjust your goals and ensure they remain meaningful and fulfilling.

Setting Goals for Personal Development and Well-Being

Personal development and well-being goals focus on your overall growth as an individual. These goals can include improving your mental and physical health, building self-confidence, developing positive habits, and fostering meaningful relationships. Here's how to set goals for personal development and well-being:

1. **Focus on Holistic Growth**: Personal development is about growing in all areas of your life. Think about the qualities you want to develop, such as resilience, empathy, or self-discipline. Consider goals that will help you become a more well-rounded person, such as practicing mindfulness, improving your fitness, or volunteering in your community.
2. **Set Goals for Mental Health and Self-Care**: Taking care of your mental health is just as important as achieving academic or extracurricular success. Set goals that prioritize self-care, such as setting aside time for relaxation, practicing gratitude, or engaging in activities that bring you joy and reduce stress.

3. **Develop Positive Habits**: Personal development often involves creating and maintaining positive habits. Identify habits you want to build or improve, such as getting regular exercise, eating healthy, getting enough sleep, or practicing good time management. Set goals that help you incorporate these habits into your daily routine.
4. **Foster Healthy Relationships**: Building and maintaining strong, positive relationships is a key aspect of personal development. Set goals that focus on strengthening your connections with friends, family, and peers. This might involve improving your communication skills, being more supportive, or spending quality time with loved ones.
5. **Monitor Your Well-Being**: Regularly check in with yourself to see how you're feeling and whether your personal development goals are contributing to your overall well-being. Use tools like journaling or self-assessment quizzes to track your progress and adjust as needed.

Kaylie's Diverse Goals: Balancing Academics, Sports, and Personal Growth

Kaylie's journey to improving her math grade was just one part of her broader goal-setting strategy. She also set goals for her extracurricular activities and personal development, aiming to create a well-rounded plan that supported her growth in multiple areas. Here's how Kaylie balanced her diverse goals:

1. **Academic Goals**: Kaylie's primary academic goal was to raise her math grade from a C to an A. She set specific milestones, created a study plan, and used various resources like tutoring and study groups to achieve her goal. By setting a clear academic goal, Kaylie stayed focused on her studies and made consistent progress.
2. **Sports Goals**: In addition to her academic goals, Kaylie was passionate about soccer. She set a goal to improve her skills as a midfielder and earn a starting position on her school's team. To achieve this, Kaylie practiced regularly, attended extra training sessions, and sought feedback from her coach. Balancing her soccer commitments with her academic responsibilities required careful time management and prioritization.
3. **Personal Development Goals**: Kaylie also set goals for personal growth, including improving her self-confidence and managing stress more effectively. She practiced mindfulness and meditation, made time for hobbies she enjoyed, and worked on developing positive relationships with her peers and family members. These goals helped Kaylie maintain a healthy balance between her academic, extracurricular, and personal life.

By setting diverse goals and using effective strategies to achieve them, Kaylie was able to create a balanced and fulfilling plan for her growth and development. Her experience demonstrates the importance of setting goals in multiple areas of your life and finding ways to balance

Worksheet: Creating Goals for Different Areas of Your Life

Use this worksheet to set goals for different areas of your life. Think about what you want to achieve academically, in your extracurricular activities and hobbies, and in your personal development and well-being.

1. Academic Goals:

- What specific academic goals do you want to achieve? (e.g., improve a particular grade, develop a new study habit, learn a new skill)

My Academic Goals:

_____

_____

_____

_____

_____

What steps will you take to achieve these goals? (e.g., create a study schedule, seek help from a tutor, join a study group)

Steps to Achieve My Academic Goals:

_____

_____

_____

_____

2. Extracurricular and Hobbies Goals:

- What are your goals for your extracurricular activities or hobbies? (e.g., improve a skill, participate in a competition, learn a new activity)

My Extracurricular and Hobbies Goals:

_____

_____

_____

_____

_____

_____

- How will you balance these goals with your academic responsibilities? (e.g., time management strategies, prioritizing tasks)

Balancing Extracurricular and Academic Goals:

_____

_____

_____

_____

_____

_____

3. Personal Development and Well-Being Goals:

- What personal development or well-being goals do you want to set? (e.g., improve mental health, develop positive habits, build stronger relationships)

My Personal Development and Well-Being Goals:

_____

_____

_____

_____

_____

- What actions will you take to support these goals? (e.g., practice mindfulness, create a self-care routine, set relationship-building activities)

Actions to Support My Personal Development and Well-Being Goals:

_____

_____

_____

_____

_____

4. Reflect on Your Goals:

- How do these goals align with your overall vision for your life? How will achieving these goals help you grow and develop?

Reflection on My Goals:

_____

_____

_____

_____

_____

Journaling Prompt: Think about the different areas of your life where you've set goals. How do these goals contribute to your overall growth and development? How do you feel about the balance between these areas?

_____

_____

_____

_____

_____

_____

_____

_____

_____

_____

_____

_____

_____

_____

_____

_____

_____

_____

_____

_____

_____

_____

_____

Setting goals in different areas of your life helps create a balanced, fulfilling approach to personal growth and development. By focusing on academics, extracurricular activities, and personal well-being, you can ensure that you're growing in all aspects of your life and achieving a well-rounded sense of accomplishment. Remember, the key to successful goal setting is finding balance and staying committed to your plans. Let's continue this journey together, setting and achieving diverse goals that help you become the best version of yourself!

Chapter 10: Long-Term Goal Planning and Vision Setting

Setting goals is an essential part of achieving success, but not all goals are created equal. Some goals are short-term and can be achieved in a few weeks or months, while others are long-term and require years of planning, dedication, and effort. Long-term goal planning is about envisioning your future and creating a roadmap to get there. This chapter will explore the difference between long-term and short-term goals, the power of vision boards in goal setting, and provide activities to help you visualize and plan your future. We'll also look at how Kaylie used a vision board to set her long-term goals and stay motivated.

Understanding Long-Term vs. Short-Term Goals

Before diving into the specifics of long-term goal planning, it's important to understand the difference between long-term and short-term goals and how they complement each other.

1. **Short-Term Goals**:
   o **Definition**: Short-term goals are objectives that you can achieve relatively quickly, usually within a few days, weeks, or months. These goals are often stepping stones toward your long-term goals and help you make steady progress.
   o **Examples**: Studying for an upcoming test, learning a new skill over the summer, completing a project for school, or joining a club or sports team.
   o **Purpose**: Short-term goals help you stay focused, provide immediate motivation, and allow you to see quick results. They're essential for building momentum and maintaining motivation as you work toward your larger objectives.
2. **Long-Term Goals**:
   o **Definition**: Long-term goals are broader objectives that take more time to achieve—often several years or even decades. These goals require planning, perseverance, and a clear vision of what you want to accomplish in the future.
   o **Examples**: Graduating from college, becoming fluent in a new language, saving money for a big purchase, or pursuing a career in a specific field.
   o **Purpose**: Long-term goals give you a sense of direction and purpose. They help you focus on the big picture and guide your decisions and actions over an extended period. Achieving long-term goals often requires breaking them down into smaller, manageable steps and consistently working toward them.

By setting both short-term and long-term goals, you can create a balanced plan that allows you to achieve immediate successes while working steadily toward your bigger dreams.

Creating a Vision Board

A vision board is a powerful tool for long-term goal setting and vision planning. It's a visual representation of your dreams and aspirations, filled with images, quotes, and words that inspire you and reflect what you want to achieve in your life. Here's how creating a vision board can help you set and achieve your long-term goals:

1. **Clarifies Your Goals**: A vision board helps you clarify what you truly want by encouraging you to think deeply about your long-term goals and dreams. The process of selecting images and words that resonate with you forces you to articulate your desires and intentions.
2. **Keeps You Motivated**: By placing your vision board somewhere visible, such as on your wall or desk, you're constantly reminded of your goals and dreams. This daily visual cue keeps you motivated and focused, even when you face challenges or setbacks.
3. **Encourages Positive Thinking**: Vision boards are filled with positive, inspiring images and messages that reinforce a positive mindset. This can help you stay optimistic and resilient, especially when working toward long-term goals that require sustained effort and dedication.
4. **Acts as a Blueprint for Your Future**: A vision board serves as a visual blueprint for your future. It helps you see the bigger picture and understand how your current actions contribute to your long-term goals. This clarity can guide your decision-making and ensure you're consistently moving in the right direction.
5. **Promotes Accountability**: Sharing your vision board with friends, family, or a mentor can create a sense of accountability. When others know what you're working toward, you may feel more committed to following through on your goals.

Kaylie's Vision Board Example: Dreaming Big and Planning Ahead

Kaylie found that creating a vision board was a transformative experience in her journey to achieving her long-term goals. Here's how she approached her vision board and what it included:

1. **Identifying Her Long-Term Goals**: Kaylie started by identifying her long-term goals, which included graduating with honors, playing soccer in college, and becoming a successful entrepreneur. She wanted her vision board to reflect these aspirations and inspire her to take action every day.
2. **Choosing Inspiring Images and Quotes**: Kaylie gathered magazines, printed images from the internet, and collected quotes that resonated with her goals. She selected images that represented her desired outcomes, like a graduation cap for her academic goals, a soccer ball for her athletic aspirations, and a picture of a businesswoman for her

entrepreneurial dreams. She also included quotes like "Dream big, work hard" and "Success is no accident" to motivate her.

3. **Organizing Her Vision Board**: Kaylie organized her vision board into sections, each representing a different aspect of her life. This helped her visualize how her goals were interconnected and reinforced the idea that achieving balance was crucial for long-term success.

4. **Reflecting and Revising**: As Kaylie continued to work toward her goals, she periodically revisited her vision board to reflect on her progress. If her goals evolved or she achieved certain milestones, she updated her vision board to reflect her current aspirations. This kept her vision board relevant and aligned with her evolving dreams.

5. **Using Her Vision Board Daily**: Kaylie placed her vision board in a spot where she would see it every day, such as above her desk. This daily reminder kept her focused and motivated, reinforcing her commitment to her long-term goals and encouraging her to take consistent action.

Kaylie's vision board was more than just a collage of pictures—it was a powerful tool that helped her stay motivated, maintain clarity, and keep her dreams front and center in her daily life.

Activity: Craft Your Own Vision Board

Creating your own vision board is a fun and creative way to visualize your long-term goals and keep yourself motivated. Follow these steps to craft a vision board that reflects your dreams and aspirations.

Instructions:

1. **Gather Your Materials**: You'll need a board or large piece of paper, magazines, printed images, scissors, glue, markers, and any other decorative items you like (stickers, glitter, etc.).

2. **Identify Your Long-Term Goals**: Take some time to think about your long-term goals. What do you want to achieve in the next 5, 10, or 20 years? Consider all areas of your life, including academics, career, relationships, personal growth, and well-being.

My Long-Term Goals:

_____

_____

3. **Find Images and Words that Inspire You**: Look through magazines or search online for images and words that represent your goals and dreams. These could be pictures of people you admire, places you want to visit, or symbols of success. Cut out or print these images and words.

4. **Arrange and Glue Your Images**: Arrange your images and words on your board in a way that feels meaningful to you. You might want to group similar goals together or place your most important goal in the center. Once you're happy with the arrangement, glue everything down.

5. **Add Personal Touches**: Use markers, stickers, or other decorative items to personalize your vision board. Write down affirmations, motivational quotes, or even a timeline for achieving your goals.

6. **Display Your Vision Board**: Place your vision board somewhere you'll see it every day, such as your bedroom, study area, or locker. This will serve as a daily reminder of what you're working toward and keep you motivated.

Reflection Questions:

1. **How did it feel to create your vision board?**

_____

_____

_____

_____

_____

2. **What do the images and words on your vision board represent?**

_____

_____

_____

_____

_____

3. **How can your vision board help you stay focused and motivated?**

_____

_____

_____

_____

_____

Journaling Prompt: After creating your vision board, write about the experience. How did it help you clarify your long-term goals? How do you feel about the future after completing this activity?

Reflection: Visualizing Your Future Self

Visualizing your future self is a powerful exercise that can help you connect with your long-term goals on a deeper level. By imagining yourself in the future, you can gain clarity on what you want to achieve and what steps you need to take to get there.

Instructions:

1. **Find a Quiet Space**: Sit in a comfortable position in a quiet space where you won't be disturbed. Close your eyes and take a few deep breaths to relax.

2. **Visualize Your Future Self**: Imagine yourself 5, 10, or 20 years from now. Picture what your life looks like—where are you living? What are you doing? Who are you with? Think about the goals you've achieved and how you feel about your life.

3. **Focus on the Details**: Pay attention to the details of your future life. What are your surroundings like? What emotions do you feel? What values and qualities have helped you achieve your goals? The more vivid your visualization, the more powerful the exercise will be.

4. **Reflect on Your Visualization**: After a few minutes, open your eyes and take some time to reflect on your visualization. Write down what you saw, how you felt, and any insights you gained.

Reflection on My Future Self:

_____

_____

_____

_____

_____

_____

_____

_____

_____

_____

_____

_____

_____

_____

5. **Set Intentions Based on Your Visualization**: Based on your visualization, set intentions for how you will start working toward your long-term goals. What actions will you take? What habits will you build? Write down your intentions and keep them somewhere you can review regularly.

My Intentions for Achieving My Long-Term Goals:

_____

_____

_____

_____

_____

_____

_____

Journaling Prompt: How did visualizing your future self-help you connect with your long-term goals? What steps can you take today to start moving toward the future you envisioned?

_____

_____

_____

_____

_____

_____

_____

_____

Long-term goal planning and vision setting are crucial components of achieving the life you desire. By understanding the difference between short-term and long-term goals, creating a vision board, and visualizing your future self, you can create a clear and inspiring roadmap for your future. Remember, achieving your dreams takes time, effort, and persistence, but with a strong vision and a commitment to your goals, anything is possible. Let's continue this journey together, setting long-term goals and working toward the future you've always imagined!

Chapter 11: Revisiting and Adjusting Your Goals

Setting goals is an important step in achieving success, but it's equally crucial to revisit and adjust them as you grow and circumstances change. Life is unpredictable, and sometimes the path to reaching your goals isn't as straightforward as you'd like. This chapter will explore why revisiting your goals is essential, how to adjust them without feeling like a failure, and provide real-life examples of teens who successfully adapted their goals. We'll also offer a worksheet to help you review and adjust your current goals.

Why Revisiting Goals is Crucial

Goals aren't meant to be set in stone. Revisiting your goals regularly ensures they remain relevant and aligned with your evolving priorities, interests, and circumstances. Here's why it's crucial to revisit your goals:

1. **Ensures Relevance and Alignment**: Over time, your interests, values, and circumstances can change. Revisiting your goals allows you to ensure they still align with who you are and what you want to achieve. It's important to have goals that reflect your current passions and priorities.
2. **Helps You Stay Motivated**: If your goals no longer excite or motivate you, it's a sign that they may need to be adjusted. Regularly revisiting your goals keeps them fresh and inspiring, helping you stay motivated and engaged in your pursuit.
3. **Allows for Flexibility and Adaptability**: Life can be unpredictable, and obstacles or opportunities can arise that you didn't anticipate when setting your goals. Revisiting your goals allows you to be flexible and adapt to new situations, ensuring you stay on the right path to success.
4. **Encourages Reflection and Growth**: Reflecting on your progress toward your goals provides valuable insights into what's working well and what could be improved. This self-reflection encourages personal growth and helps you develop strategies to overcome challenges and achieve your goals.
5. **Prevents Burnout**: Sticking to a rigid goal that no longer serves you can lead to frustration and burnout. Revisiting your goals ensures that you're focusing your energy on what truly matters, preventing feelings of overwhelm and keeping you energized.

How to Adjust Goals Without Feeling Like a Failure

Adjusting your goals doesn't mean you've failed; it's a natural and healthy part of the goal-setting process. Here's how to adjust your goals without feeling like a failure:

1. **Recognize That Change is Part of Growth**: Understand that as you grow and learn, your goals will evolve. Changing your goals to reflect your current reality isn't a failure—it's a sign of maturity and self-awareness.
2. **Focus on the Learning Experience**: Instead of viewing a change in your goals as a setback, see it as an opportunity to learn and grow. Reflect on what you've learned from your experiences and how this new knowledge can help you set more meaningful and achievable goals.
3. **Acknowledge Your Progress**: Even if you haven't achieved a specific goal, recognize the progress you've made along the way. Every step you take is valuable and contributes to your growth. Celebrate your efforts and the skills you've developed, regardless of the outcome.
4. **Adjust Goals Based on New Information**: Sometimes, you set goals with the best intentions but realize later that they aren't realistic or aligned with your true desires. It's okay to adjust your goals based on new information and insights. This shows that you're adaptable and willing to make changes to better yourself.
5. **Set Smaller, Achievable Milestones**: If a goal feels too overwhelming or unattainable, break it down into smaller, more manageable milestones. This approach allows you to make steady progress and feel a sense of accomplishment along the way.

Kaylie's Adjustments: Learning from Mistakes and Adapting

Kaylie's journey to improving her math grade and achieving her other goals wasn't without its challenges. Along the way, she faced setbacks and had to adjust her goals to stay on track. Here's how Kaylie adapted and learned from her experiences:

1. **Facing Unexpected Challenges**: Kaylie initially set a goal to improve her math grade from a C to an A by the end of the semester. However, she encountered unexpected challenges, such as difficulty understanding complex concepts and time management issues with her extracurricular activities.
2. **Reflecting on What Wasn't Working**: Kaylie took time to reflect on what wasn't working in her original plan. She realized that her study methods weren't effective for her learning style and that she needed more support in understanding certain topics.
3. **Adjusting Her Goal and Strategy**: Instead of giving up on her goal, Kaylie adjusted her approach. She set a more realistic goal of raising her grade to a B first, then working toward an A. She also sought additional help from a tutor and revised her study schedule to allocate more time for math.

4. **Learning from Mistakes**: Kaylie viewed her need to adjust her goals as a learning experience. She understood that making changes was necessary for her growth and that adapting her goals didn't mean she had failed. This mindset helped her stay positive and focused on her progress.

5. **Celebrating Small Wins**: As Kaylie worked toward her adjusted goals, she celebrated each small win, such as understanding a challenging concept or improving her test scores. These celebrations kept her motivated and reinforced her belief in her ability to succeed.

Kaylie's story shows that adjusting your goals based on your experiences and new information is a smart and effective approach. By remaining flexible and open to change, you can continue to grow and achieve your dreams.

Case Studies: Teens Who Adjusted Their Goals and Found Success

Let's look at a few more examples of teens who adjusted their goals and found success. These stories highlight the importance of flexibility and resilience in goal setting:

Case Study 1: Jordan's Academic Turnaround

Jordan set a goal to get straight A's during his sophomore year. However, he struggled with a particularly challenging science class and saw his grades slipping. Instead of feeling defeated, Jordan adjusted his goal to focus on mastering the subject rather than getting an A. He sought extra help from his teacher, used additional resources, and gradually improved his understanding of the material. By the end of the year, he was proud of his progress and had developed a love for science he hadn't expected.

Case Study 2: Maya's Sports Journey

Maya wanted to make the varsity basketball team, but during tryouts, she realized she wasn't as prepared as she thought. Instead of giving up, Maya adjusted her goal to improve her skills over the next year and try out again. She joined a local league, attended skills camps, and practiced regularly. The following year, not only did she make the varsity team, but she also became one of its key players.

Case Study 3: Ethan's Personal Growth

Ethan set a goal to read one book a week for a year. After a few months, he found it hard to keep up due to his busy schedule. Rather than feeling like he'd failed, Ethan adjusted his goal to reading for 30 minutes every day, regardless of how many books he finished. This new goal was more sustainable, and Ethan discovered a deeper enjoyment of reading without the pres

These case studies show that adjusting your goals based on your experiences can lead to unexpected successes and personal growth. It's about finding what works for you and being willing to change course when necessary.

Worksheet: Reviewing and Adjusting Your Current Goals

Use this worksheet to review and adjust your current goals. Reflect on your progress, identify what's working well, and consider any changes you may need to make.

1. Review Your Current Goals:
- List your current goals and reflect on your progress. Are you on track? What successes have you achieved so far?

My Current Goals:

_____

_____

_____

Reflection on Progress:

_____

_____

_____

2. Identify What's Working and What's Not:
- What strategies and actions have been effective in helping you achieve your goals? What challenges or obstacles have you encountered?

What's Working:

_____

_____

_____

What's Not Working:

_____

_____

_____

_____

_____

4. **Adjust Your Goals if Needed**:

- Based on your reflection, do you need to adjust any of your goals? Consider whether your goals are still relevant, realistic, and aligned with your current priorities.

Adjusted Goals:

_____

_____

_____

Reasons for Adjustment:

_____

_____

_____

5. **Create a New Action Plan**:

- Develop a new action plan for achieving your adjusted goals. Include any new strategies or resources you plan to use.

New Action Plan:

_____

_____

_____

6. **Set a Date to Revisit Your Goals**:

- Choose a date in the near future to revisit your goals and assess your progress. Regularly reviewing your goals ensures they remain relevant and achievable.

Date to Revisit Goals: _____

Journaling Prompt: How do you feel about adjusting your goals? What have you learned from this process, and how will it help you achieve future goals?

_____

_____

_____

_____

_____

_____

_____

_____

_____

Revisiting and adjusting your goals is an essential part of the goal-setting process. It allows you to stay flexible, learn from your experiences, and remain focused on what truly matters. Remember, adjusting your goals doesn't mean you've failed; it means you're growing, adapting, and becoming more in tune with your journey. Let's continue to embrace change and stay committed to achieving our dreams, no matter what obstacles come our way!

Chapter 12: Goal Setting Beyond High School

As you approach the end of high school, it's time to start thinking about what comes next. Whether you're planning to go to college, enter the workforce, or pursue other paths, setting goals for your future is key to preparing for this new chapter of your life. This chapter will guide you in setting meaningful goals for college, career, independence, and adult life. We'll also look at Kaylie's future plans and provide activities to help you map out your post-high school goals and reflect on what you want to achieve in the next five years.

Preparing for College and Career Goals

Transitioning from high school to college or a career is a major life change, and having clear goals can help you navigate this new terrain more effectively. Here's how to set goals for college and career success:

1. **Research Your Options**: Start by exploring different colleges, programs, and career paths that align with your interests and strengths. Consider what you're passionate about and where you see yourself in the future. Researching your options will help you set informed goals that align with your aspirations.
2. **Set Specific Academic and Career Goals**: If you're planning to attend college, set goals related to your field of study, desired grades, extracurricular involvement, and any other academic achievements. For career goals, think about the type of job you want, the skills you need to develop, and any internships or work experience that will help you get there.
3. **Plan for the Application Process**: If college is your next step, set goals for each stage of the application process. This might include researching schools, preparing for entrance exams, writing personal statements, and meeting application deadlines. Breaking down the process into manageable steps will make it feel less overwhelming.
4. **Build a Network and Seek Guidance**: Start building a network of mentors, teachers, career counselors, and professionals in your field of interest. Seek advice and guidance from people who can help you understand the path you're interested in and provide support as you set and achieve your goals.
5. **Prepare Financially**: Whether you're heading to college or starting a career, financial preparation is important. Set goals for saving money, applying for scholarships or financial aid, and budgeting for expenses. Financial planning will help you start your next chapter with confidence and security.

Setting Goals for Independence and Adult Life

Transitioning to adult life involves more than just academic and career preparation; it also includes setting goals for independence, personal growth, and life skills. Here's how to set goals for becoming a successful and independent adult:

1. **Develop Life Skills**: Set goals to develop essential life skills, such as cooking, budgeting, time management, and basic home maintenance. These skills will help you live independently and manage your daily responsibilities effectively.
2. **Plan for Living Arrangements**: If you're planning to move out on your own, set goals for finding a suitable place to live, understanding lease agreements, and budgeting for rent and utilities. Consider whether you want to live with roommates or alone and what steps you need to take to secure your ideal living situation.
3. **Build a Support Network**: As you transition to independence, having a support network of friends, family, and mentors is crucial. Set goals for maintaining strong relationships with those who support you and can offer guidance as you navigate adult life.
4. **Focus on Health and Well-Being**: Set goals for maintaining your physical and mental health as you become more independent. This could include developing a regular exercise routine, eating a balanced diet, managing stress, and seeking support when needed.
5. **Explore Personal Growth Opportunities**: Beyond academics and career, think about other areas of personal growth you want to pursue. This could include traveling, volunteering, learning a new language, or pursuing a hobby or passion. Setting goals in these areas will help you develop a well-rounded and fulfilling life.

Kaylie's Plans for the Future: Setting Goals Beyond High School

Kaylie has always been a goal-setter, and as she prepares for life after high school, she's focusing on several key areas to ensure a smooth transition to adulthood. Here's how Kaylie is setting goals for her future:

1. **College Preparation**: Kaylie plans to attend a university with a strong business program. Her goals include researching potential schools, maintaining her grades, and preparing for college entrance exams. She has also set a goal to apply for several scholarships to help cover tuition costs.
2. **Career Exploration**: Interested in entrepreneurship, Kaylie is setting goals to gain real-world experience through internships and part-time jobs in her desired field. She's also networking with local business owners and seeking mentorship to learn more about the industry.

3. **Developing Independence**: To prepare for independent living, Kaylie is setting goals to learn essential life skills such as budgeting, cooking, and time management. She's also planning to save a portion of her earnings from a summer job to help cover her living expenses in college.

4. **Personal Growth and Well-Being**: Kaylie knows that personal growth is just as important as academic and career success. She's setting goals to maintain her physical and mental health, stay active in sports, and continue her involvement in community service. These goals will help her stay balanced and well-rounded as she transitions to adulthood.

5. **Building a Supportive Network**: Recognizing the importance of a strong support system, Kaylie is setting goals to stay connected with friends and family while also building new relationships in college and her career field. She plans to join clubs and organizations that align with her interests and values to expand her network.

Kaylie's thoughtful approach to setting goals beyond high school illustrates the importance of planning for all aspects of your future, from education and career to personal growth and independence.

Activity: Map Out Your Post-High School Goals

This activity will help you create a roadmap for your life beyond high school. Take some time to think about your future and map out your goals in various areas.
Instructions:

1. **Identify Your Key Areas of Focus**: Think about the different areas of your life that are important to you as you transition out of high school. This might include college, career, personal development, independence, and health.

   Key Areas of Focus:

   _____

   _____

   _____

2. **Set Specific Goals for Each Area**: For each area of focus, set one or more specific goals. Be sure to make your goals S.M.A.R.T. (Specific, Measurable, Achievable, Relevant, and Time-bound).

College/Career Goals:

_____

_____

_____

Independence Goals:

_____

_____

_____

Personal Development Goals:

_____

_____

_____

Health and Well-Being Goals:

_____

_____

_____

3. **Create an Action Plan**: Write down the steps you need to take to achieve each goal. Consider any resources or support you might need and set a timeline for each step.

Action Plan for My Goals:

_____

_____

_____

_____

4. **Visualize Your Future**: Take a few minutes to close your eyes and visualize yourself achieving each of these goals. What does your life look like? How do you feel? Visualization can help reinforce your commitment to your goals and keep you motivated.

_____

_____

_____

Journaling Prompt: How does it feel to plan your future? What are you most excited about, and what challenges do you anticipate? How will you overcome them?

_____

_____

_____

Reflection: What Do You Want to Achieve in the Next Five Years?
Reflecting on where you want to be in the next five years can help you set long-term goals and create a vision for your future. Use this reflection exercise to think about your aspirations and how you can achieve them.

Instructions:

1. **Reflect on Your Aspirations**: Think about where you want to be in five years. What do you want to have accomplished academically, professionally, and personally? Write down your thoughts.

In the Next Five Years, I Want to Achieve:

_____

_____

_____

2. **Identify the Steps to Get There**: What steps do you need to take to achieve these goals? Consider the skills you need to develop, the experiences you want to gain, and the support you'll need along the way.

Steps to Achieve My Five-Year Goals:

_____

_____

_____

3. **Set Milestones**: Break your five-year goals into smaller milestones that you can achieve along the way. Setting milestones will help you stay on track and maintain motivation.

Milestones for My Five-Year Goals:

_____

_____

_____

_____

4. **Reflect on Potential Challenges**: What challenges might you face in achieving these goals? How can you prepare for them and stay resilient?

Potential Challenges and Solutions:

_____

_____

_____

Journaling Prompt: Reflect on your five-year plan. How does it align with your values and passions? What are you most excited about, and what are you most nervous about?

_____

_____

_____

Setting goals for life beyond high school is an exciting opportunity to shape your future and pursue your dreams. By preparing for college and career, setting goals for independence, and reflecting on what you want to achieve, you can create a roadmap for success and fulfillment. Remember, this is your journey, and with the right goals and mindset, you have the power to create the future you envision. Let's continue this journey together, setting goals that lead you to a bright and promising future!

Chapter 13: Building a Lifelong Goal-Setting Habit

Goal setting isn't just a one-time activity—it's a lifelong practice that helps you grow, adapt, and achieve your dreams. Whether you're working on personal development, career aspirations, or other aspects of your life, setting and pursuing goals keeps you focused and motivated. This chapter explores why goal setting should be a lifelong habit, offers tips for maintaining your goal-setting routine, shares Kaylie's advice on keeping up with goal setting as you grow, and includes activities to help you continue setting goals throughout your life.

Why Goal Setting Should be a Lifelong Practice

Setting goals throughout your life is crucial for several reasons. Here's why goal setting should be a consistent habit:

1. **Encourages Continuous Growth**: Life is a journey of continuous learning and self-improvement. Setting goals helps you push your boundaries, learn new skills, and grow both personally and professionally. By regularly setting goals, you ensure that you're always moving forward and developing as a person.
2. **Provides Direction and Purpose**: Having goals gives you a sense of direction and purpose. It helps you stay focused on what's important to you and provides a roadmap for where you want to go. Whether it's short-term or long-term, having clear goals prevents you from drifting aimlessly and keeps you aligned with your values and aspirations.
3. **Builds Resilience and Adaptability**: Life is full of unexpected changes and challenges. Regularly setting and revising goals helps you build resilience and adaptability. When you're used to setting goals, you're more prepared to handle setbacks, adjust your plans, and find new paths to success.
4. **Enhances Motivation and Satisfaction**: Achieving goals, no matter how big or small, gives you a sense of accomplishment and boosts your motivation. This ongoing cycle of setting, working toward, and achieving goals leads to greater satisfaction and fulfillment in life.
5. **Helps You Prioritize Your Time and Energy**: With countless opportunities and distractions in life, setting goals helps you prioritize where to focus your time and energy. It ensures that you're dedicating your resources to what truly matters and aligns with your long-term vision.

Tips for Maintaining Your Goal-Setting Routine

Keeping up with goal setting can be challenging, especially as life gets busy. Here are some tips to help you maintain a consistent goal-setting routine:

1. **Set Regular Check-Ins**: Schedule regular check-ins with yourself to review your goals and progress. This could be monthly, quarterly, or annually—whatever works best for you. Use these check-ins to reflect on what's working, what's not, and what adjustments you need to make.
2. **Use a Goal Journal or Planner**: Keep a dedicated goal journal or planner where you write down your goals, track your progress, and reflect on your experiences. This can help you stay organized and make it easier to see your growth over time.
3. **Break Goals into Smaller Steps**: Large goals can feel overwhelming, so break them down into smaller, more manageable steps. This makes it easier to stay focused and motivated, and allows you to celebrate small wins along the way.
4. **Stay Flexible and Open to Change**: Be willing to adjust your goals as needed. Life is unpredictable, and sometimes your goals will need to evolve with your circumstances. Staying flexible and open to change will help you stay resilient and adaptable.
5. **Celebrate Your Achievements**: Take time to celebrate your successes, both big and small. Celebrating achievements boosts your confidence and motivation, and reinforces the value of setting and pursuing goals.
6. **Seek Support and Accountability**: Share your goals with friends, family, or mentors who can provide support and hold you accountable. Having a support system can help you stay motivated and committed to your goals.
7. **Reflect on Your Why**: Regularly remind yourself why you set your goals in the first place. Reflecting on your motivations and passions helps you stay connected to your purpose and reinforces your commitment to your goals.

Kaylie's Tips for Keeping Up with Goal Setting as You Grow

As Kaylie has grown and achieved her goals, she's developed several strategies for maintaining her goal-setting routine. Here are Kaylie's top tips for keeping up with goal setting throughout your life:

1. **Create a Vision for Your Future**: Kaylie found that having a clear vision for her future made it easier to set meaningful goals. She regularly revisits her vision board and updates it to reflect her evolving dreams and aspirations. This helps her stay focused on what's important and motivates her to keep setting and achieving new goals.

2. **Be Realistic About Your Capacity**: Kaylie learned that it's important to be realistic about what she can achieve, especially when life gets busy. She sets goals that challenge her but are still attainable, allowing her to make steady progress without feeling overwhelmed.

3. **Embrace Failure as a Learning Opportunity**: Kaylie views failure as a natural part of the goal-setting process. When things don't go as planned, she reflects on what went wrong, learns from her mistakes, and adjusts her goals accordingly. This mindset helps her stay positive and resilient, even when faced with setbacks.

4. **Stay Organized and Focused**: To stay on top of her goals, Kaylie uses a planner to organize her tasks, track her progress, and set deadlines. She also sets aside dedicated time each week to work on her goals, ensuring that she stays focused and committed.

5. **Keep Your Goals Visible**: Kaylie keeps her goals visible by writing them down and placing them somewhere she can see every day, such as on her desk or in her journal. This constant reminder helps her stay motivated and keeps her goals at the forefront of her mind.

6. **Regularly Reassess and Adjust Your Goals**: Kaylie understands that goals aren't set in stone. She regularly reassesses her goals to ensure they're still relevant and aligned with her current priorities. If a goal no longer serves her, she isn't afraid to adjust or replace it with a new one.

By following these tips, Kaylie has been able to maintain a consistent goal-setting routine that supports her growth and success.

Worksheet: Setting Monthly and Yearly Goals

Use this worksheet to set both monthly and yearly goals. Regularly setting goals helps you stay focused, motivated, and aligned with your long-term vision.

1. Set Your Monthly Goals:

- Think about what you want to achieve this month. What are the most important goals you want to focus on? Write down your top three-monthly goals and the steps you'll take to achieve them.

My Monthly Goals:

_____

_____

Steps to Achieve My Monthly Goals:

_____

_____

_____

2. Set Your Yearly Goals:

- Reflect on what you want to achieve over the next year. Consider all areas of your life, including academics, career, personal development, and well-being. Write down your top three yearly goals and the steps you'll take to achieve them.

My Yearly Goals:

1. _____
2. _____
3. _____

Steps to Achieve My Yearly Goals:

1. _____
2. _____
3. _____
4. _____
5. _____

_____

_____

_____

3. Plan Your Check-Ins:

- Set dates for when you'll check in on your goals and assess your progress. Regular check-ins help you stay on track and adjust as needed.

Monthly Check-In Date:

_____

Yearly Check-In Date:

_____

4. Reflect on Your Goals:

- Take a moment to reflect on why these goals are important to you and how they align with your long-term vision. Write down your thoughts.

Reflection on My Goals:

_____

_____

_____

_____

_____

Journaling Prompt: How do your monthly and yearly goals contribute to your overall growth? What steps will you take to ensure you stay committed to these goals?

_____

_____

_____

_____

_____

Reflection Activity: The Importance of Continuous Growth

Reflecting on the importance of continuous growth helps you stay committed to lifelong goal setting. Use this activity to think about how ongoing growth impacts your life and future.

Instructions:

1. **Reflect on Your Growth Journey**: Think about how much you've grown over the past year, five years, or even longer. What goals have you achieved, and how have they shaped who you are today?

   Reflection on My Growth Journey:

   _____

   _____

   _____

   _____

   _____

2. **Identify Areas for Future Growth**: Consider areas where you'd like to continue growing and developing. What skills, habits, or experiences do you want to pursue in the future?

Areas for Future Growth:

_____

_____

_____

_____

Set a Growth Mindset: Write down a mantra or affirmation that encourages continuous growth and goal setting. Use this mantra to stay motivated and focused on your journey.

My Growth Mindset Mantra:

_____

_____

_____

Journaling Prompt: Why is it important to commit to continuous growth? How will setting and revisiting goals help you achieve your long-term vision?

_____

_____

_____

_____

_____

Building a lifelong goal-setting habit is essential for ongoing growth, adaptability, and success. By regularly setting and revisiting goals, maintaining a consistent routine, and staying open to change, you can continue to evolve and achieve your dreams. Remember, goal setting is a journey, not a destination, and every step you take brings you closer to becoming the best version of yourself. Let's keep moving forward together, setting goals that inspire and drive you toward a bright future!

As you reach the end of this book, it's time to reflect on everything you've learned about setting and achieving your goals. Goal mastery is a journey that requires persistence, dedication, and a willingness to adapt. Let's recap some of the key takeaways, offer final words of encouragement, share some inspirational quotes, and discuss what's next on your path to continuous learning and growth. Finally, Kaylie will share a note about her ongoing journey, reminding you that this is just the beginning.

Conclusion

Recap of Key Takeaways

1. **Understand the Power of Goals**: Goals are more than just dreams—they are actionable plans that give you direction and purpose. They help you focus on what matters most and motivate you to strive for your best.

2. **Set S.M.A.R.T. Goals**: Specific, Measurable, Achievable, Relevant, and Time-bound goals are crucial for success. They provide a clear roadmap and make it easier to track your progress and stay on course.

3. **Embrace a Growth Mindset**: Believing in your ability to learn and grow is fundamental to achieving your goals. A growth mindset helps you view challenges as opportunities and setbacks as learning experiences.

4. **Build a Support Network**: Surround yourself with people who support your goals and encourage your growth. Whether it's friends, family, mentors, or teachers, having a strong support network is key to staying motivated and resilient.

5. **Celebrate Small Wins and Reflect**: Recognizing your achievements, no matter how small, keeps you motivated. Regularly reflecting on your progress helps you learn from your experiences and adjust your goals as needed.

6. **Stay Flexible and Adaptable**: Life is full of unexpected changes, and your goals may need to evolve with them. Being willing to adjust your goals without feeling like a failure is essential for long-term success.

7. **Commit to Lifelong Goal Setting**: Goal setting is not just a one-time activity; it's a lifelong practice that keeps you moving forward. Continue to set, revisit, and adjust your goals throughout your life to ensure continuous growth and development.

Final Words of Encouragement

Remember, the journey to mastering your goals is a personal one. There will be highs and lows, moments of triumph and times of doubt. What's important is that you keep going. Each step you take, each goal you set and achieve, brings you closer to becoming the person you want to be. Believe in yourself, trust the process, and know that you have the power to shape your future.

Stay curious, stay determined, and don't be afraid to dream big. Your goals reflect your potential, and with perseverance and the right mindset, there's no limit to what you can achieve. As you continue on this journey, remember that you are capable, strong, and worthy of every success.

Inspirational Quotes and Messages

To help keep you motivated, here are some inspirational quotes and messages to remind you of the power of goal setting:

1. **"The future belongs to those who believe in the beauty of their dreams."** – Eleanor Roosevelt
   Believe in your dreams and trust that you have what it takes to make them a reality.
2. **"Success is not final, failure is not fatal: It is the courage to continue that counts."** - Winston Churchill
   Keep pushing forward, no matter the setbacks. Each step forward is progress.
3. **"You are never too old to set another goal or to dream a new dream."** – C.S. Lewis
   Goal setting is a lifelong journey. Embrace it with an open heart and a curious mind.
4. **"Believe you can, and you're halfway there."** - Theodore Roosevelt
   Confidence in yourself and your abilities is half the battle. Trust in your journey.
5. **"The only limit to our realization of tomorrow is our doubts of today."** – Franklin D. Roosevelt
   Let go of doubt and embrace the possibilities that lie ahead.

Use these quotes to inspire you on challenging days and remind you of the strength and determination within you.

What's Next? Encouraging Continuous Learning and Growth

Your journey doesn't end here. In fact, this is just the beginning. Continue to set new goals, learn from your experiences, and push yourself to grow in ways you never thought possible. Here are a few ways to keep moving forward:

1. **Stay Curious and Open to New Experiences**: Always be open to learning and trying new things. Embrace opportunities that challenge you and expand your horizons.
2. **Set New Challenges Regularly**: Don't be afraid to step out of your comfort zone. Setting new challenges helps you grow and keeps life exciting.
3. **Reflect and Adjust**: Regularly reflect on your goals and adjust them as needed. Growth is a dynamic process, and being willing to adapt is key to continuous development.
4. **Seek Out Mentors and Role Models**: Learn from those who have walked the path before you. Mentors and role models can provide valuable guidance and inspiration.
5. **Celebrate Every Milestone**: No matter how big or small, every achievement is worth celebrating. Take time to acknowledge your progress and reward yourself for your hard work.

Remember, growth is a continuous journey, not a destination. Keep learning, keep striving, and keep believing in your ability to achieve your dreams.

A Note from Kaylie: Her Journey Continues

Hi there! It's Kaylie again. I hope my story has inspired you to start your own journey toward goal mastery. Remember, I started just like you, unsure of what I wanted to achieve and how to get there. Through setting goals, staying focused, and adapting along the way, I discovered so much about myself and what I'm capable of.

I want you to know that this is just the beginning for both of us. Even after achieving many of my goals, I continue to set new ones and push myself to grow. Life will always bring new challenges and opportunities, and that's what makes the journey so exciting.

As you move forward, stay true to yourself and what you want to achieve. Keep your goals in sight, but also be kind to yourself when things don't go as planned. Every step you take, even the small ones, brings you closer to your dreams.

Thank you for joining me on this journey. I'm excited to see what amazing things you will accomplish. Remember, you have the power to shape your future—believe in yourself and go for it!

With all my best wishes,
Kaylie

Congratulations on completing this book and taking the first steps toward mastering your goals. Remember, the power to achieve your dreams is in your hands. Keep setting goals, keep striving, and most importantly, keep believing in yourself. The journey to goal mastery is ongoing, and with each step, you're growing into the incredible person you're meant to be.

Now, go out there and turn your dreams into reality!

Appendix

The appendix is filled with extra resources and tools to help you continue your journey to goal mastery. Here, you'll find additional worksheets and templates to support your goal-setting process, a list of recommended resources, inspirational quotes and affirmations to keep you motivated, and contact information for mentorship and support. Plus, we have a special planner and vision board kit available to help you stay organized and inspired!

Additional Worksheets and Templates

To help you further develop your goals and track your progress, here are some extra worksheets and templates. You can print them out and use them as often as needed:

1. **Daily Goal Tracker**: A template to plan and track your daily goals, helping you stay focused on what needs to be accomplished each day.
2. **Weekly Reflection and Review Sheet**: A worksheet to help you reflect on your week's progress, celebrate your successes, and identify areas for improvement.
3. **Monthly Goal Planner**: A template to outline your goals for each month, along with actionable steps to achieve them and deadlines to keep you on track.
4. **Year-End Reflection Worksheet**: A guided worksheet to review the past year, reflect on what you've learned, and set new goals for the coming year.
5. **Overcoming Obstacles Worksheet**: A tool to help you identify potential challenges, develop strategies to overcome them, and stay resilient in the face of setbacks.

Feel free to customize these templates to fit your unique needs and preferences. The more you use them, the more effective your goal-setting routine will become!

Recommended Resources: Books, Apps, and Websites

Here are some recommended resources to help you continue learning about goal setting, personal growth, and motivation:

Books:

- *"Atomic Habits" by James Clear*: Learn how to build good habits and break bad ones with practical strategies for everyday life.
- *"The 7 Habits of Highly Effective Teens" by Sean Covey*: A great guide for teens on how to manage their time, goals, and relationships effectively.
- *"Grit: The Power of Passion and Perseverance" by Angela Duckworth*: Discover the importance of perseverance and how to develop a growth mindset.

Apps:

- **Habitica**: Turn your goal setting into a game! Track your habits and daily goals in a fun and interactive way.
- **Trello**: An app for organizing tasks, setting goals, and managing projects with visual boards and checklists.
- **Forest**: A unique app that helps you stay focused on your goals by growing a virtual tree for every task you complete without distractions.

Websites:

- **MindTools.com**: Offers a range of resources for personal and professional development, including goal-setting strategies.
- **Coursera.org**: Access free courses on personal development, productivity, and more from top universities around the world.
- **TeenHealth.org**: Provides articles and tips on managing stress, setting goals, and maintaining a healthy balance in life.

These resources are excellent for expanding your knowledge and finding new ways to stay motivated and on track with your goals.

Inspirational Quotes and Affirmations to Keep You Motivated

Here's a collection of motivational quotes and affirmations to inspire you on your journey to goal mastery. Use them as daily reminders to keep pushing forward:

1. **"The only way to achieve the impossible is to believe it is possible."** – Charles Kingsleigh
   Believe in yourself and your ability to overcome challenges.
2. **"Start where you are. Use what you have. Do what you can."** – Arthur Ashe
   Every small step counts. Begin your journey with what you have today.
3. **"Success is not how high you have climbed, but how you make a positive difference to the world."** – Roy T. Bennett
   Focus on making a positive impact, and success will follow.

Daily Affirmations:

- "I am capable of achieving my goals and dreams."
- "Every day, I am growing stronger, smarter, and more confident."
- "I embrace challenges as opportunities to learn and grow."
- "I am focused, determined, and unstoppable."

Write these affirmations down, repeat them to yourself daily, and let them fuel your motivation.

Contact Information for Mentorship and Support

Building a support network is crucial for achieving your goals. Here are some resources for finding mentorship and support:

1. **School Counselors and Teachers**: Reach out to your school counselors and teachers who can offer guidance and help you connect with resources for goal setting and personal development.
2. **Local Community Centers**: Many community centers offer programs and workshops focused on youth development, career exploration, and mentorship. Check your local center's offerings and get involved.
3. **Online Mentorship Programs**: Websites like **Mentor.org** and **Big Brothers Big Sisters** offer virtual mentorship programs that connect you with mentors who can guide you in achieving your goals.
4. **Youth Organizations**: Organizations such as **4-H**, **Boys & Girls Clubs of America**, and **YMCA** provide programs that promote leadership, personal growth, and goal-setting skills.
5. **Social Media Groups**: Join online communities on platforms like Facebook or LinkedIn where you can connect with like-minded individuals and seek advice from mentors in your area of interest.

Don't hesitate to reach out for support. Having a mentor or a supportive community can make a huge difference in your journey to achieving your goals.

Special Bonus: Planner and Vision Board Kit

To help you stay organized and inspired on your goal-setting journey, we're excited to offer a **Planner and Vision Board Kit** as a special bonus with this book!

The Planner Includes:

- **Daily, Weekly, and Monthly Planning Pages**: Keep track of your goals, appointments, and to-do lists with easy-to-use planning pages designed to help you stay focused and productive.
- **Goal-Setting Templates**: Dedicated sections for setting S.M.A.R.T. goals, tracking your progress, and reflecting on your achievements.
- **Habit Tracker**: Monitor your daily habits and routines to ensure you're consistently working toward your goals.

The Vision Board Kit Includes:

- **Vision Board Template**: A ready-to-use template to create your personalized vision board. Fill it with images, quotes, and affirmations that inspire you and represent your dreams.
- **Motivational Stickers and Cut-Outs**: A variety of stickers and cut-outs to decorate your vision board and planner with empowering messages and visuals.
- **Guided Exercises**: Step-by-step exercises to help you clarify your vision, set meaningful goals, and create a board that motivates you daily.

With this **Planner and Vision Board Kit**, you'll have all the tools you need to keep your goals front and center, stay organized, and stay motivated on your journey to success. Whether you're setting academic, personal, or career goals, this kit will help you stay on track and keep moving forward.

Thank you for being a part of this journey to goal mastery. Remember, you have the power to shape your future, and with the right tools, mindset, and support, anything is possible. Keep striving, keep growing, and never stop believing in your ability to achieve great things. The world is yours—go out and make it happen!

1. Daily Goal Tracker

Daily Goal Tracker

| Date: _____ |

Daily Goal Action Steps Deadline Progress Notes
1.
2.
3.

Reflection Questions:

- What went well today?

_____

_____

_____

- What could I improve on tomorrow?

_____

_____

_____

Use this template each day to plan and track your goals. Reflect on your progress and adjust your action steps as needed.

2. Weekly Reflection and Review Sheet

| Week of:
_____|

1. Achievements This Week:
- What did I accomplish this week?
    1.
    2.
    3.

3. Challenges Faced:

- What challenges did I encounter?
    1.
    2.
    3.

3. Lessons Learned:

- What did I learn from these experiences?
    1.
    2.

4. Areas for Improvement:

- What can I improve next week?
    1.
    2.

5. Goals for Next Week:

- What are my top goals for next week?
    1.
    2.
    3.

Use this sheet at the end of each week to reflect on your progress, celebrate your achievements, and plan for the week ahead.

3. Monthly Goal Planner

Monthly Goal Planner

| Month: _____ |

Goal Action Steps Deadline Progress Notes
1.
2.
3.

Reflection Questions:

- What are my priorities for this month?
- What resources or support do I need to achieve these goals?

Use this at the beginning of each month to set your goals, outline the steps needed to achieve them, and reflect on your progress.

4. Year-End Reflection Worksheet

Year-End Reflection Worksheet

| Year: _____ |

1. Major Achievements:

- What were my biggest accomplishments this year?
    1.
    2.
    3.

2. Lessons Learned:

- What lessons did I learn this year?
    1.
    2.

3. Challenges and How I Overcame Them:

- What challenges did I face, and how did I overcome them?
    1.
    2.

4. Areas for Improvement:

- What areas do I want to improve next year?
    1.
    2.

5. Goals for the New Year:

- What are my top goals for the new year?
    1.
    2.
    3.

Use this worksheet at the end of each year to review your achievements, reflect on what you've learned, and set new goals for the upcoming year.

5. Overcoming Obstacles Worksheet

Overcoming Obstacles Worksheet

| Date: _____ |

1. Identify the Obstacle:

- What challenge am I facing?

2. Analyze the Obstacle:

- Why is this challenge difficult for me?

3. Brainstorm Solutions:

- What are some possible ways to overcome this obstacle?
    1.
    2.
    3.

4. Create an Action Plan:

- What specific steps will I take to overcome this obstacle?
    1.
    2.
    3.

5. Set a Timeline:

- When will I take these steps?

6. Reflection:

- How did I feel after working through this challenge?

- What did I learn from this experience?

References

Books

Covey, S. R. (2014). *The 7 Habits of Highly Effective Teens*. Simon & Schuster.

Duckworth, A. (2016). *Grit: The Power of Passion and Perseverance*. Scribner.

Clear, J. (2018). *Atomic Habits: An Easy & Proven Way to Build Good Habits & Break Bad*

   Ones. Avery.

Journal Articles

Locke, E. A., & Latham, G. P. (2002). Building a practically useful theory of goal setting and task motivation: A 35-year odyssey. *American Psychologist, 57*(9), 705-717.

Moeller, A. J., Theiler, J. M., & Wu, C. (2012). Goal setting and student achievement: A longitudinal study. *The Modern Language Journal, 96*(2), 153-169.

Websites and Online Resources

MindTools. (n.d.). *How to set goals: Goal setting techniques from MindTools.com.* https://www.mindtools.com/pages/article/newHTE_90.htm

Mentor.org. (n.d.). *Become a Mentor*. https://www.mentor.org

Reports and Manuals

National Academy of Sciences. (2017). *Integrating goals into education and training: A report for educators and policymakers*. National Academies Press.